SPEAKING OF STEWARDSHIP

SPEAKING OF STEWARDSHIP

Model Sermons on Money and Possessions

WILLIAM G. CARTER
editor

GENEVA PRESS
LOUISVILLE, KENTUCKY

Book and cover design by Jennifer K. Cox

First Edition
Published by Geneva Press
Louisville, Kentucky

This book is printed on acid-free paper that meets the American National Standards Institute Z39.48 standard. ∞

PRINTED IN THE UNITED STATES OF AMERICA
98 99 00 01 02 03 04 05 06 07 — 10 9 8 7 6 5 4 3 2 1

Library of Congress Cataloging-in-Publication Data

Speaking of stewardship : model sermons on money and possessions/
    William G. Carter, editor, — 1st ed.
        p.   cm.
    Includes bibliographical references.
    ISBN 0-664-50031-5 (alk. paper)
    1. Stewardship, Christian.   2. Stewardship, Christian—Sermons.
3. Sermons, American.   I. Carter, William G., 1960-
BV772.S634   1998
248'.6—dc21   98-4050

Contents

Preface

Issuing a book of stewardship sermons on the eve of the new century is a brave undertaking. The church is slowly coming to realize that stewardship questions are at the heart of contemporary discipleship. News outlets daily remind us that North Americans consume natural resources at a rate far in excess to our proportion of the world's population. "International economic development" at times is a description of removing natural resources for use in developed nations. The implications for discipleship are enormous.

Our culture is often described as "consumerist," admitting to overwhelming efforts to convince us we need to buy more and more, to "upgrade" so we can "be on the cutting edge of style." Yet scripture tells us we cannot serve both God and mammon. The gap between the haves and the have-nots continues to grow. While people in some parts of our world live comfortably with adequate food and housing, elsewhere the refugee population swells. Children die unnecessarily from contaminated water, from eradicable diseases, and from starvation. Yet scripture tells us we are called on to serve those in such desperate need.

Writers and other leaders in science, anthropology, and religion join forces to protest a constantly growing overuse of natural resources, leading to destructive pollution and land waste. Yet scripture tells us that God looked at creation and declared it "good."

Escape through drug and alcohol substance abuse destroys people's physical and mental lives. Yet scripture tells us our bodies are a "temple of the Spirit."

The guides and examples for preaching about stewardship in this book demonstrate that we cannot separate faithful use of God's gifts from concerns for justice and compassion. The preachers who have contributed their work are persons who understand their craft as part of the continuing dialogue between the Word of God and the people of God. They understand that preaching about stewardship confronts concerns of faith and wealth, of environment, of vocation, and of many other demands of discipleship.

This is an important book. It gives clarity to a subject too long trivialized as institutional support. Readers will find in it inspiration and guidance for one of the most critical issues in the church today.

David McCreath

Coordinator, Stewardship Education
Presbyterian Church (U.S.A.)

Contributors

SUSAN R. ANDREWS is the pastor of Bradley Hills Presbyterian Church, Bethesda, Maryland. She received a Doctor of Ministry degree from McCormick Theological Seminary and served as Chair of the Call System Task Force for the General Assembly.

WILLIAM G. CARTER serves as pastor of First Presbyterian Church, Clarks Summit, Pennsylvania. A jazz pianist, college music lecturer, and trustee of Princeton Theological Seminary, Bill served as the general editor of this project.

TERRY L. CHAPMAN is the pastor of Roseland Presbyterian Church, Roseland, New Jersey. He is currently pursuing a Doctor of Ministry degree in Spirituality from San Francisco Theological Seminary.

GEORGE CHORBA serves as pastor of First Presbyterian Church, New Vernon, New Jersey. George has long been recognized within the PC(USA) as a mentor for new pastors. He received a Doctor of Philosophy degree from New York University.

FRED B. CRADDOCK was selected as one of the top twelve preachers in the English-speaking world in an international survey conducted by Baylor University. In his retirement from a distinguished career in teaching homiletics at Candler School of Theology, Fred regularly volunteers as a preaching instructor in rural Appalachia. His sermon is transcribed from a speaking occasion at Columbia Theological Seminary, and is included by his permission, but without the benefit of his editing.

PAUL DEBENPORT is pastor of First Presbyterian Church, Albuquerque, New Mexico. A native Texan, and proud of it, Paul is a trustee of Austin Theological Seminary and a blues guitarist.

ROBERT J. ELDER, pastor of First Presbyterian Church, Salem, Oregon, is the author of more than forty published articles and sermons. He is a classically trained tenor soloist. Rob assisted with editorial tasks for this project.

CAROL ANN FLEMING is co-pastor of Park Central Presbyterian Church, Syracuse, New York. A former staff member of the Synod of the Northeast, Carol received a Doctor of Ministry degree from Columbia Theological Seminary.

ROGER P. HOWARD serves as pastor of Sharon Community Presbyterian Church, Moon Township, Pennsylvania. Roger is an airplane pilot and EMT in his spare time.

WILLIAM R. LEETY is pastor of Overbrook Presbyterian Church, Columbus, Ohio. A poet whose work regularly appears in *The Presbyterian Outlook*, Bill assisted with editorial tasks for this project.

JAMES E. MEAD serves as pastor of University Place Presbyterian Church, Tacoma, Washington. In recognition of his distinguished service to the Presbyterian Church (U.S.A.), Jim was selected as vice moderator of the 210th General Assembly (1998).

VIRGINIA MINER serves as pastor of Calvin United Presbyterian Church, Olyphant, Pennsylvania, and First Presbyterian Church of Peckville, Pennsylvania. An advocate for social justice and peacemaking concerns, Virginia went with Witness for Peace to Nicaragua in 1987 and was an election observer with Pastors for Peace in 1990.

JAMES MOISO is pastor of Westminster Presbyterian Church, Portland, Oregon. Jim has served on the board of trustees of San Francisco Theological Seminary, where he also received a Doctor of Ministry degree and chaired the seminary's alumni/ae council.

CHARLES L. RICE is Professor of Homiletics in the Theological School, Drew University, Madison, New Jersey, and is assisting priest at St. John's Episcopal Church, Montclair.

ROBERT RICHARDSON is pastor of the Marple Presbyterian Church, Broomall, Pennsylvania. Bob is a beloved and effective minister to youth, and a Certified Christian Educator in the PC(USA). He cur-

rently serves as secretary on the Educator Certification Council of the
General Assembly.

WANDA SEVEY is pastor of First Presbyterian Church, Delanco, New Jersey. She is a clinical member of the American Association for Marriage and Family Therapy and enjoys reading mystery novels.

ARTHUR E. SUNDSTROM serves as pastor of Chevy Chase Presbyterian Church, Washington, D.C. Art has been active in the Presbyterian Peacemaking Program and chaired the Bicentennial Fund committee for his synod.

THOMAS H. TROEGER is professor of preaching and communications at Iliff School of Theology, Denver, Colorado. A master flutist and author of numerous hymns, Tom has written widely on the role of the imagination in preaching.

CARLOS E. WILTON, pastor of Point Pleasant Presbyterian Church, Point Pleasant Beach, New Jersey, received a Doctor of Philosophy degree in Divinity from the University of St. Andrews, Scotland. Formerly assistant dean and director of admissions of the University of Dubuque Theological Seminary, he moderates the "Preaching Stewardship" electronic meeting on the Presbynet/Ecunet computer network.

INTRODUCTION
Speaking of Stewardship

William G. Carter

In my first church, the boxes had been barely unloaded from the moving truck when a church member informed me that the second Sunday of November was designated as Stewardship Sunday. "This year we need some inspiration," he said. "Last summer was a lean season for the church coffers, and we want the congregation to afford our brand-new pastor."

As a child of the Presbyterian Church, I knew what he expected. Every week my father wrote out a check for the church while my mother was hustling the four kids out to the car for Sunday school. While we sat in worship, Dad would often reward the quietest child by letting him or her put the envelope in the offering plate. My parents, both church officers, made yearly visits for the every-member canvass in my home church. And we knew what Stewardship Sunday was all about. Once a year, like it or not, we heard a financial pitch from our church's pulpit. It always happened between Halloween and Thanksgiving.

And so, five weeks after my ordination as a minister of Word and Sacrament, I preached my first stewardship sermon. I had no idea what I was doing. The lectionary served up a Gospel lesson from Mark about the poor widow who dropped two coins in the offering box. That seemed like a good text, so I nailed together a sermon on it. When Sunday came, I stood to read my manuscript. A huge pulpit hid my quivering knees. It was quickly evident as I looked at my bleary-eyed congregation that this sermon, despite my best intentions, was sinking to the members' worst expectations.

If I had missed their reactions during the service, it would have been confirmed by comments after worship.

The first response came from the church treasurer, a retired military officer. He said, "That was the worst stewardship sermon I ever heard." When I picked myself off the floor, he continued, "You didn't mention the budget once. Even worse, you didn't make anybody feel guilty."

Another member was more earnest. "Pastor," he said, "thank you for your sermon today. I was anxious when I saw the bulletin board on the street corner. It announced today was Stewardship Sunday, but your sermon calmed my fears."

I breathed a sigh of relief and asked, "Did I say something helpful?"

"Better than that," he said. "Reverend, today you didn't say anything at all!"

The most helpful feedback, however, came from one of the saintly members of the church, a woman well known for her deep piety and encouraging disposition. She stopped me at coffee hour and thanked me for my "good effort." Then she added, "I wish you had preached that sermon a few weeks ago."

"Thank you," I said, "but why?"

"Most of us filled out our pledge cards before we came to church today," she replied. "If you preached that sermon a few weeks ago, some of us might have increased our pledges."

"You know," I countered, "you can always give more than the amount that you write on your card."

"I don't think so," she said with a sly smile. "I always fill out my pledge card in red ink."

Thinking about it, the three greatest challenges to stewardship preaching are evident in those responses.

First, the church treasurer expected a sermon about underwriting the institutional church. The bottom line for him? Meeting the budget! He assumed the church's primary aim on earth is to pay its bills, meet its current commitments, and maintain the status quo. The primary means of institutional enforcement is a sermon that tells people to get in line and pay up. If this goal can be served by laying some guilt upon a captive congregation, then it is the preacher's job to do so.

In this scenario, where is the laughter of generosity? The joy of Christian faith? The expectation of God's surprising and abundant harvest? All have evaporated—because of a lack of vision.

Second, the church member who claimed that I said nothing was probably on the mark, as I can now see when I read over those early sermons. Some congregations may be prone to a suffocating institutionalism, but there are also some preachers like me who don't know what to say about stewardship. We may be well spoken on all kinds of theological issues and social concerns, but we develop a form of laryngitis when the pledge cards are passed out. Pastors who are normally clear stumble at this point and lose themselves in platitudes and generalities. Some people in our pews may lack ears to hear, but many preachers lack a voice when it comes to speaking of stewardship. Dare we ask for money? How do we do it? What language shall we borrow? Frankly, we don't know. And the seminaries did not have time to teach us.

Third, and perhaps most important, there is the issue of an ongoing pastoral relationship. Yes, timing is essential. A wise preacher plans ahead and should make an appeal before expecting a response. Yet I had been on the job for only five weeks. At that early juncture, what did I know about the people who worshiped in that church?

Christian pastors live among the people of their churches. They share the same dreams for their children, shop in the same stores, and stand for the same neighborhood concerns. The Sunday sermon gives a weekly opportunity to deepen the relationship between pulpit and pew. The preacher has an obligation—and a regular privilege—to address important issues from the pulpit. If a complex matter like stewardship is merely scheduled as an annual sermon topic, we ignore it as a daily concern of every Christian disciple. It matters what we do with our God-given money, time, and talents. If we let the institutional calendar be the sole determining factor of when we will speak of stewardship, our preaching lacks intentionality.

The stakes are even higher for those of us who live in North America in the last years of the twentieth century. In our time and place, there is no greater challenge than speaking of Christian stewardship. Our culture is marked by deep anxiety and late-night fear. People are immobilized by lost jobs and failed hopes. Afraid that the world suffers from a scarcity of resources, otherwise generous people will hoard what they have and install security systems in a vain attempt to feel secure.

We swim in a sea of consumerism, which threatens to swallow up the life we share. One prevailing icon is the shopping mall. An artificial community of anonymous purchases has replaced the village square, where the consumer has been separated from the producer. In the mall, seasons are marked, not by the weather or the church calendar, but by the passing of holiday buying seasons. Communication is reduced to public service announcements and blue-light specials. People are gathered by the experience of making a purchase, assuming, of course, they are able to buy things; that explains why the poor are shooed away from the shopping mall. Consumers come and go as autonomous individuals, without any sense of interdependence or shared life. By the time they return to the parking lot, they are tempted to believe that their purchases will solve all their problems.

In a time of buying power, we lose our sense of gratitude. Our children think they are entitled to a toy every time they roll through the fast-food drive-through. And many believe it is a sign of culturally blessed individualism to have something that others do not.

The result: consumerism erodes our humanity. Like the character in Jesus' parable, we build bigger barns to keep our stuff secure, and we find ourselves increasingly unable to lead simple lives, choosing clutter and confusion, often against our better judgment.

The answer? We will speak of stewardship. We will proclaim the economy of God, an interconnected system of relationships inaugurated by the word and work of Jesus Christ. We will preach the love of God, which makes no distinction between rich and poor, yet finds its expression in justice and shalom for all. We will name the deep hungers of the human condition and offer a satisfying banquet of hope that cannot be purchased, only received as a holy gift. We will talk about human responsibility as the primary response to God's generosity.

In short, we will speak of stewardship. And we will speak on a regular basis. To this end, let me suggest ten characteristics of a good stewardship sermon.

1. *A good stewardship sermon should be a good sermon.* Every time we climb into a pulpit, we are called upon to do our best work, to the glory of God. Nothing shoddy or ill-prepared will do. For about twenty minutes on a Sunday morning, we offer the finest fruits of our study and prayer so that the people before us might hear a Word from God. A stewardship sermon is neither a sales pitch nor an appeal for institutional self-preservation. It is a sermon, defined as "an oral interpretation of the written Word of scripture for a community of baptized people who have gathered to worship the Triune God." And it should be a good one.

According to Fred Craddock, a good sermon has six features:

> a unified theme that gives confidence to the preacher and clarity to the listeners;
>
> a "memory" that sets the sermon within the tradition of the believing community;
>
> a nod of recognition that precedes any shock of recognition;
>
> a quality of identification with the human situation that draws in listeners;
>
> a form that creates and sustains anticipation;
>
> an intimacy between speaker and hearer that is supported by an oral presentation.[1]

2. As mentioned above, *a good stewardship sermon is part of a continuing conversation between a preacher and a congregation.* While an annual sermon

in early November may get the attention of some listeners, it is usually too little too late. A sustained pastoral relationship invites us regularly to wrestle with things that matter. Certainly this includes money and our use of it. Our love for God and our ongoing concern for the people in the congregation are the two best reasons to speak of stewardship.

If we talk about money for only a Sunday or two in the fall, then Christian stewardship starts to sound like fund-raising. We must not diminish the fullness of what it means to be managers of God's entire household. In baptism, we are commissioned to tend to God's economy twelve months a year. God gives us a multitude of gifts in order to participate in the divine order. We need fifty-two weeks in a row to get our responsibilities straight and our priorities in order. It's hard work, yet absolutely essential for the life of the world. How dare we talk about the "S" word only once a year—and then do so sheepishly?

3. *A good stewardship sermon is clear about its intention.* Every preacher must ask, "What does this sermon intend to do?" The question is not merely "What do I want to say?" but "What do I want to accomplish by the time I sit down?"

If we speak about stewardship only once a year, our intention may be reduced to an appeal for the budget, a justification of the session's financial decisions, or (at worst) a defense of the preacher's raise. Are those the only tasks we wish to accomplish? I think not. Let the preacher offer regular stewardship sermons that intend to:

> wrestle with demanding scripture texts and their implications for our pocketbooks
>
> engage listeners in a theological conversation about the place of money and possessions in our lives
>
> undermine thoughtless consumerism with simplicity and gratitude
>
> give folks a chance to choose the God of liberation over the idol of Mammon
>
> cultivate a habit of generosity
>
> enlarge our little worlds with a glimpse of the world as God sees it
>
> encourage the financial discipleship of those present (we can't preach to those absent!)
>
> teach about the benefits of making and keeping commitments, financial and otherwise
>
> offer wise counsel on personal money management

challenge people to take care of gifts already entrusted to them

reflect on our daily work as a primary arena of faithfulness

remind people that "Jesus saves" is not the slogan of a local bank, but an act of costly love that "demands my soul, my life, my all"

request money . . . for God's sake!

4. *A good stewardship sermon is, in its own way, countercultural,* particularly among those who sense they have been exiled to the foreign land of consumerism. An effective preacher will provide a critique of prevailing views on money, acquisitiveness, and security and offer an alternative vision of God's reign. Preachers in our culture may want to listen to Walter Brueggemann, who describes our North American context this way:

> It is a world of cynical indifference that is geared to indulgence, aimed at satiation, and powered by greed. In political language, it is called "opportunity," but the ideology of "yuppies" (and most of their parents from whom they learned) is to get all you can, live an uninterrupted life of well-being without respect to others, pay as little tax as possible (none for the public welfare), join nothing, make no commitments, and let others get along and get ahead as best they can.[2]

Is this a picture of the good life? Or does it name our pain? Do we want to live unto ourselves or for others? Are we born in order to consume or to share? Is life intended to be a series of VISA transactions or a repeating invitation to wean ourselves from false attachments? Preacher, you decide . . . and speak up!

5. *A good stewardship sermon is biblical in its content and form.* The Bible is the sourcebook for understanding and participating in God's economy. Every time we want to talk about love or peace or justice or grace, we open the Bible and it starts talking about stewardship. The Book will not let us off the hook. In terms of content, the Bible's concerns must become the preacher's concerns. The primary subject of a good stewardship sermon is God, who creates and redeems a good world, claims and judges a people who are commissioned to be responsible, and moves us toward the day when all manner of things shall be redeemed.

What about form? The preacher can take some homiletical cues from the ways that the Bible speaks. We hear stories about the uninhibited generosity of others (Ex. 35:4–36:7; 2 Chron. 31:1–10), prophetic denunciations of affluence (Amos 4:1–2; James 5:1–6), concerns and guidelines for property and promised land (any number of texts from the Pentateuch), warnings about the snares and false dependencies of this life

(Matt. 6:19–21, 24–33), to say nothing of direct invitations and well-worded appeals (Rom. 15:22–29). Paul is the foremost stewardship preacher in the New Testament, and we are fortunate to have a nearly complete sermon within the Corinthian correspondence (2 Corinthians 8—9). Paul invites people to join him in a "generous undertaking," fully aware that a heavy-handed demand would not receive a whole-hearted response. Our sermons will bear fruit if they speak in the many voices that the scriptures speak.

6. *A good stewardship sermon will ask for money when it is appropriate to do so.* If we do not ask for money, we cannot expect it to be given. Ministers have an endless number of excuses for why they dance around the topic without making a direct solicitation. Not least among these is the nagging sense that the preacher asks people to pledge to God, knowing that some of the funds will pay the preacher.[3]

Nevertheless, something must be said. Ponder the comment of a frustrated churchgoer. One Sunday she exclaimed to her ambiguous pastor, "Why don't you tell me what you want me to do?" It's good advice. Preachers of stewardship must not get lost in vague generalities and unspecified requests. They must not assume that everybody else knows what they are talking about. Use direct language. Make clear requests. Go through a sermon manuscript and cross out every line that leads you away from what you really want to say.

7. *A good stewardship sermon is both globally responsible and inescapably local.* A stewardship preacher names the local congregation's work and interprets it through the global view of our Creator. We seek to understand the larger work of God, particularly as it addresses the economic powers and principalities.

Yet the sermon is necessarily local. Preachers will not be embarrassed by local references or concrete images, especially if they highlight and promote the work of the risen Christ. God may be at work in all things for those who love him (Rom. 8:28), but God is also busy somewhere. It is the preacher's job to tell those stories. When people catch a glimpse of what God is doing in their backyard, they will give all that they have to possess that holy field. The preacher, then, is an interpreter of God's neighborhood, in both its enormousness and specificity.

8. *A good stewardship sermon normally speaks in the tone of first-person plural* ("we" and "us"). All of us are addressed by the Word and Spirit of God. When it comes to giving money (or anything else), preachers must not lay burdens upon their hearers that they themselves will not carry. I, for one, am tired of preachers who brag about tithing. I am repulsed by preachers who do not pledge.

Let the preachers come down from their high horses and preach to the best capacities in the people who listen to them. Let us refuse the temptation to manipulate, coerce, point fingers, or otherwise blast good Christian people out of their pews. Let us dare to talk about our own struggles with money and gratitude.

And from one preacher to another: let us identify concerns in the life of our congregations that we will quietly underwrite.

9. *A good stewardship sermon is aware of its social location.* The context shapes the hermeneutic. So here's the critical question: Where is this sermon preached? To a struggling single mother in the trailer park? To the CEO of the regional bank? To the migrant worker in the cinder block bunkhouse? To the up-and-coming couple who are suffocated by a huge mortgage? All of them attend my church, and each of them hears a vastly different sermon on the same Sunday morning. Socially speaking, it matters where the pulpit is located, and the wise preacher knows it.

For instance, in the fifth chapter of James, the preacher stands up to wail against the rich: "Your gold and silver have rusted, and their rust will be evidence against you, and it will eat your flesh like fire (James 5:1–6)." Surprisingly, New Testament commentators believe James said those words to a poor congregation. The rhetorical form is an "apostrophe," a speech to people who are *not* present. In this way, Brother James comforts his impoverished church with the reassurance that the coming of the Lord will set things right. Commenting on this hermeneutical dynamic, Tom Long writes,

> The effect of this reading upon the contemporary respondent will depend, of course, upon where that reader is positioned. For those Christian groups who today suffer at the hands of the rich and powerful, the text speaks again its word of encouragement. If, poetically speaking, we are in the Manor House, we hear the strong warnings coming from the little church, but we also "overhear" the word of promise to the disadvantaged congregation. All of these levels of meaning in the text allow for a variety of sermonic approaches, none of them alike, but all of them faithful to this text.[4]

10. *A good stewardship sermon encourages gratitude to God,* who is greater than we know and more generous than we have eyes to see. In the New Testament, the activity of God is so profound that the same word is used for both the giving and the receiving of the gift. The word is *charis,* which is translated "grace." As Craddock has written, "The word may refer to a favor shown or a favor received. [It] may define an act of giving or an act of receiving: if giving, the word means 'gift or unearned favor'; if receiving, then the word is best translated 'gratitude.' Since the same term represents both sides of the act, it is natural to expect that grace as gift would

be met with grace as gratitude."[5] Either way, giving or receiving, here is a glimpse of the economy of God!

Gratitude is a gift to receive as well as a virtue to pursue. We don't have anything to give, except as we have received. Every breath of life, every heartbeat, every conscious thought is a gift. Every person we meet, every friend we make, every relationship that warms the heart and challenges the soul is a gift. Every opportunity to work, every meaningful task, every dollar earned is a gift. Our lifelong task is learning how to respond to grace with graciousness. In the meantime, poet George Herbert invites us to pray with him:

> Thou that hast given so much to me,
> Give one thing more: a grateful heart.[6]

With this volume, a number of like-minded preachers intend to provide a helpful resource for the ecumenical church. Most of the authors belong to the Homiletical Feast, a collegial group of Presbyterian ministers who gather annually to prepare for preaching. Charles Rice, Tom Troeger, and Fred Craddock are special friends of this group. The Homiletical Feast is thankful to God for their sage wisdom, so freely given on many occasions, and for their generosity, which permits us to share their sermons with a wider audience. Such graciousness exemplifies the spirit of Christian stewardship. We also recognize the abundant support of Tom Long, who has also taken part in our annual gatherings, and who has offered enthusiasm for this volume through his role as director of Geneva Press. Like his homiletician colleagues, Tom has been a continuing source of insight, clarity, and helpful criticism. We are grateful to God for his gifted ministry.

The sermons in this book deal with a diversity of scripture texts, with a slight bias toward passages that appear in the ecumenical lectionary. The authors approach the biblical texts with a full awareness of contemporary trends in homiletics, which means, among other things, that there are no sermons of the "three points and a poem" variety. We also recognize that sermons, by definition, are spoken events in congregation worship. While translating these sermons into a print medium, we have made every attempt to maintain their original oral character.

The authors believe stewardship is a twelve-month concern for Christian disciples, and not merely an annual appeal for institutional funding. That's why we offer sermons on the place of money in our lives, the myth of global scarcity, the spirituality of generosity, and the economy of God. It is our hope that the breadth of topics will nudge our colleagues to address their congregations on similar issues.

As this book was developed, we were struck by the fact that effective stewardship sermons are necessarily bound to the life and circumstances of a local congregation. There is no such thing as a generic stewardship sermon, cleaned up in publication for all people everywhere. As Lesslie Newbigin reminds us, "the only hermeneutic of the gospel is a congregation of men and women who believe it and live by it."[7] Therefore, some of the following sermons have local references, thereby offering encouragement for our colleagues to speak about things that truly matter to their congregations. We hope the good word of stewardship will be spoken, and that it might be believed and lived by Christians on the edge of a new millennium.

THEOLOGICAL DIMENSIONS
OF STEWARDSHIP

GOOD CIRCULATION
Daniel 5:23

Thomas H. Troeger

You have praised the gods of silver and gold, . . . which do not see or hear or know; but the God in whose power is your very breath, and to whom belong all your ways, you have not honored. (Daniel 5:23)

It was not a loud sound.
But it was persistent.
Bang. Bang. Bang. Bang. Bang.
I figured it was a noisy forced-air heating vent.
Or maybe some construction work.
But having just awakened from the anesthetic,
I wanted it to stop.
Bang. Bang. Bang. Bang. Bang.
"O Lord," I prayed in desperation,
"Shut that thing off."
Then I realized:
it was the new artificial heart valve
the surgeon had implanted.
"Cancel that prayer, God!"
The doctor had warned me before the operation:
"It'll sound awfully loud at first,
until you get used to it."
Ever since I first heard that sound,
I have awakened each morning to pray:
"Thank you, God, my heart is beating."

A human heart is about the size of a human fist.
Lift one of your hands and make a fist.

Release it.
Clinch it.
Release it.
Clinch it.
Keep doing that for a moment while I speak.
The heart beats about sixty or seventy times a minute.
That means roughly
four thousand beats per hour.
So in an eight-hour night
your heart might beat
thirty-two thousand times!

Your hand and forearm
are probably already tired
from closing and opening your fist.
Stop.
Stop, and think about this:
last night while you were sleeping,
your heart—
without any conscious effort from you—
kept beating without a pause.
The same action that tired your hand in a minute!

And those thirty-two thousand pulse beats
sustained you only for a single night.
By the end of one week—
if we figure the much faster pulse rate of physical activity—
you might be up to a million beats.
Add up the weeks to months
and the months to your total number of years,
and then add that sum
to the sums of everyone in the congregation.

Is there anyone among us
who has gotten a bill for all of this?
I don't know any power company
that provides free service.
Surely someone will be sending us a notice:
"Dear Customer,
our records show that you are in arrears
for the beat of your heart
from the day it first started.
Pay up now or we are shutting off service."
I know now why I have always been moved
by a prayer that is frequently offered

in African American services:
"I thank you God that my bed sheet this morning
was not my winding sheet."

What wisdom in that prayer!
To realize that the mere fact of our existence
is an unearned, mysterious gift.
Every breathing,
pulse-beating second of our life
is a gift.
God's extravagance to us
exceeds every mortal thought of generosity.

And so far all I have considered
is what God has done in creating and sustaining us.
I have not yet mentioned what God has
spent to redeem us through Jesus Christ.

We know that the physical heart
pumps blood out
to pump blood in.
That's how the circulatory system works,
and if the valves or the veins become clogged,
then the heart and our circulation deteriorate.

It is a biological fact:
circulation is essential to life.
It is a spiritual fact:
circulation is essential to life.

If all we do is receive,
then we become like King Belshazzar
to whom Daniel declared:
"You have praised the gods of silver and gold . . .
which do not see or hear or know;
but the God in whose power is your very breath,
and to whom belong all your ways,
you have not honored."

"Daniel" is one of the stranger books in the Bible.
It belongs to that class of writing
that scholars call "apocalyptic,"
coming from a Greek word which means
"to bring out what is hidden,
to uncover,
to reveal."

Usually we associate such revelation
with what will happen at the end of time.
But what strikes me in this verse
is that the revelation Daniel offers in these words
is a revelation about Belshazzar's life
here and now,
about our life here and now.

At the core of our existence
is an unending process of being gifted by God—
"in whose power is our very breath."
And we are oblivious to it.
We are like Balshazzar, who Daniel says has
praised the gods of silver and gold . . .
which do not see or hear or know,
while the source of breath and pulse,
the spendthrift lover of creation
is never honored.

We go about our lives oblivious to the One
who ceaselessly lavishes us with the gift of existence.
But when the apocalyptic moment comes,
when we have our life back
after we thought we would lose it,
when we hold a newborn in our arms,
when we behold beauty that leaves us speechless,
when the realization breaks upon us
that the elemental simplicities
of breath and pulse
are gifts from God,
then
our hearts fill with gratitude,
and we become extravagant in our giving.
We wish we could give more and more and more
to thank
the infinite and eternal grace
that has allowed us to exist.

Through Our Beating Hearts Remind Us[1]
(8.7.8.7.D)

Through our beating hearts remind us
that the source of all our powers
is, O God, your vital Spirit
that is animating ours.
Every pulse beat is revealing
while we work and while we rest
that your care for us is constant
and to live is to be blest.

Yet we act as if our living
were our own accomplishment
and the purpose of creation
is whatever we invent.
We ignore the truth repeated
every second by our heart:
that our thanks should be unending
for the life your life imparts.

Brood and breathe on us your creatures
as you did upon the sea
when you split apart the darkness
and you called all things to be.
Brood and breathe and recreate us
till in Christ we are made new
and your never ending giving
is returned through us to you.

RESOURCES AT THE READY
Matthew 25:1–13

Arthur E. Sundstrom

The parable of the ten bridesmaids, a story Jesus tells near the end of his life, is not a story one often connects to the topic of stewardship. And by saying that, I've already let the cat out of the bag: this sermon is going to focus on stewardship. Stewardship Dedication Sunday is approaching, and the tradition is that the pastor will rouse you to generosity and thankfulness so that you will return your pledge cards with ever-larger gifts. And that is exactly what I plan to do.

I know the reaction this stirs up in many of you. It is best described by the little boy who was fidgeting in church one Sunday. Finally he leaned over to his mother and asked, "Mom, if we give the money now, do you think he'll let us go?" The answer is, not yet. I want to say a thing or two about the parable.

Traditionally, this story, which appears only in Matthew, is understood to be about the second coming of Jesus, the Messiah, and every detail of the story is assigned a meaning. The bridegroom? He symbolizes the returning Messiah. The bridesmaids? They represent all who await his second coming. The bridegroom's delay is what Matthew's readers were experiencing. Fifty years after the resurrection, the eagerly expected return of Christ still had not happened, and some of the believers were dying away. While the parable offered no explanation for the bridegroom's delay, it did help believers deal with it. The marriage feast is symbolic of the life to come, and the closed door, which is not opened to five bridesmaids, is the last judgment, when some are turned away.

Commentators more or less agree that every detail in this story has a hidden meaning. But, as is often the case with the parables of Jesus, some of the details in this story just don't fit into a neat explanation. For example, when the bridegroom finally does come and oil is needed by five bridesmaids, they are sent to the merchants to buy some more. But that violates logic, since merchants in the first century would not be open after dark. Also, why would the honored bridegroom suddenly take on the lowly role of door-keeper? And what about that last verse? "Keep awake therefore, for you know neither the day nor the hour." That really has little to do at all with the story at hand, since all the bridesmaids slept; none of them kept awake! That final verse actually fits more comfortably with the stories Matthew relates prior to this one, and trying to sort out all these details is really "barking up the wrong tree," so let's don't worry about the details. It is the story as a whole that rightly requires our attention.

Let's back up, then, and look at the big picture: the beginning, the middle, and the end of this story. It begins with a wonderfully gracious invitation to a party, the same kind of merciful invitation Jesus extends to the kingdom of God again and again. But in the middle, there are complications: the bridegroom is delayed, and some of the invited guests, anticipating this, are prepared with extra oil for their lamps, but others are not prepared. Finally, at the end of the story, the bridegroom appears, and the party is to begin. But those who were not prepared with extra oil are shut out of the banquet hall. They pound on the door, but to no avail. Once closed, it is closed. The kingdom of God, Jesus said, is just like that.

We like the beginning of the parable, the party setting, the open invitation to all. We can even appreciate the middle of the story, the delay—we are, after all, about to enter the third Christian millennium. But there is this inescapably difficult part, the way it ends: "the door was closed." This dire mood, this sense of finality, is why this parable isn't one of our favorite stories, because it seems to say that, even for the faithful, time can run out. Decisions must be made about discipleship, and we can't keep putting them off forever, because "forever" finally comes.

We do have to admit, though, this story accurately describes the way many of us experience our religious life. We begin with the thrill and joy of the party. We start off on our journey of faith with great enthusiasm. There are exciting days, meaningful times shared with others, and we look forward to great things happening to us in the faith. We savor every experience of living in the light of God's kingdom, and we want the Messiah to come again into our world and lives.

But then there are the delays and disappointments. We are still waiting. The Christian life is no problem if we know Jesus is coming again a week from Monday. You could bet the world would be a far different place for the next eight days. But the challenge is being a Christian every day, day after day after day after day, without knowing which day the bridegroom is going to come strolling into town; which day the big party is going to be held. It is hard to sustain faith when we are confronted with the same issues, experiences, questions, hopes, idleness, fears, and indifference as were those bridesmaids.

As the story tells us, though, there will be an ending, a day of reckoning, a time when the way we live the faith is accounted. The real question, then, is how we use this in-between time, how we live in the middle, what we make of our faith in the season of delay and struggle, this time between Jesus' first coming and Christ's return. Our choices and decisions make all the difference in the world.

And that, of course, is where stewardship comes into play. Living our faith in the in-between time means using our resources wisely. Think about that oil, so important a part of this story. Traditionally in Jewish thought and writing, oil was symbolic of good works. Now, all ten bridesmaids had oil to begin with; there were no insiders or outsiders. All had the resources to have as much oil as they needed. People were judged wise and foolish because of the way they used those resources. The wise were prepared and used those resources, in the time of waiting, to keep the faith alive, even when their expectations were not met and their hopes were tested. The foolish kept putting off the use of their resources, believing things would work out according to their timetable. They thought they could conserve their resources. "No need to use my resources for good today," they thought, "there is always tomorrow." These are the ones who counted themselves as bright and smart and savvy and had it all figured out but who ultimately are called foolish and finally find themselves shut out of the party and end up in the dark. The others, who used their resources and are often called foolish by the world, turn out to be the wise, and ultimately, the party-goers.

In this story, Matthew gives us a theology for the delay of Christ, wisdom for how we are to live a life of faith in the church in the world while we await Christ's coming. The issue is our behavior in this in-between time. As someone wrote, "It is not the coming of the bridegroom that makes some wise and some foolish; it merely reveals who is."[1]

Some of that revealing takes place every stewardship season in the church. All of us have been invited to the great celebration that awaits the faithful. And all of us certainly have been given resources to use for good in the meantime. The question is, do we use some of those resources to light the way of the coming Christ, or do we try to hold back, trying to make up excuses about why supporting good works is better done tomorrow than it is today?

Neither the church universal nor any particular congregation is perfect. But we work hard to light enough lamps so that we can glimpse what the coming celebration will be like. We work to make sure that at least some will not go to bed hungry tonight or have to rummage around to find shelter from the fall breezes. We provide some children in our town and around the world with bread and our own children a place where they know they are welcomed, loved, and accepted. We provide visits to persons who live alone and help to families going through difficult times. We proclaim God's Word and offer inspiring songs of praise in this sanctuary and rebuild homes and churches. We support great centers of learning and hospitals in this country and around the world and set up health clinics in places of need.

All of this takes resources, and you have them. And the question remains, how are you going to use them? Hoard and hold back—thinking you have the future figured out and you'll share them some other day—or do you share what you have now and so be ready for whatever God has in store for us? One of my colleagues recently told me a joke. The pastor of a Presbyterian church is standing in the pulpit speaking to the congregation. He says, "I've got good news and bad news. The good news is that we have the money for next year's budget. The bad news is it's in your pocket."

That is not really bad news; it's the truth. You have the resources necessary to support many good causes and you are asked to decide how you will use them. You have to make the choice about supporting this congregation and its work. And of course, we not only place choices before you but so do scores of other agencies and institutions who are doing good. Like the five bridesmaids who did not use their resources to buy extra oil, you can act as if extra resources for the work of the church aren't really needed, or you can choose to provide the oil that keeps the way of the coming Christ brightly lit.

GRACE AND GRAB
Luke 16:1–8

Charles L. Rice

This is one of the more difficult stories of Jesus, the story of the unjust steward. How should we interpret it?

Since most of us know, do we not, the kind of person who goes for it in life, the one who always busts a gut, we are probably inclined at first to go with John Crossan's interpretation of this parable, because it focuses on just such a character.

In Crossan's book *In Parables*, he says we should actually stop reading at verse 7, simply quit at the point where the man has negotiated with his master's debtors, "You write fifty, you write eighty." Crossan says, "Stop it right there."[1] If we do that, we are left to conclude that Jesus wants us to pay attention to this wily character who goes for it, who with clear intention covers his assets. A certain manager, the story goes, gets the word from the boss: "I've been hearing about you. It will be necessary for you to clear your desk and turn in your account books." But before he does this, while his name plate is still on the door and before it is known in the community that he is no longer in a place of authority, he calls in some debtors of his master, people who by all accounts are well-to-do in their own right, and in an endearing bid to curry favor, he acts quickly:

"How much do you owe?"

"One hundred."

"Write fifty; how much do you owe?"

"One hundred."

"Write eighty. And write quickly," he says, "before the jig is up."

Well, we know him, the guy who goes for it, and something in us admires him.

I watched the old TV show *Dallas* a couple of times, and there is some-thing in J. R. that one has to admire, a kind of singleness of purpose. He knows what he wants; he goes out to get it. We like this decisive boldness; it is so American. The alacrity of his calculations, so sure in his self-preservation.

Each of us can see it. We can see it in the teenager who feels the surge of life and, much to a parent's dismay, asserts herself or himself and seizes life, inarticulate as that teenager might be.

You remember the pivotal scene in the movie *Breaking Away;* the whole crowd in the theater cheered. What happened was that the boy finally breaks down and gets a job. (Obviously that isn't what a teenager's sup-posed to do. We probably have it all backward putting adolescents in school, keeping them indoors in springtime. Or maybe we have it all right; maybe there's just too much surging to set them loose on the street.) But, in any case, this fellow decides that he will forsake swimming in the quarry and the other joys of summer in order to take a job. So he shows up down at the used car lot; his parents are so proud. He's five minutes late and the boss lets him have it. And in finishing up with him he says, "Now kid, get out there and punch that time clock." So he goes out the door, rolling up his sleeves, and boy, does he punch it. Everybody in the theater cheered.

"It's my life—I feel it—I want it."

We know this man.

You can see it, feel it, in the energy and the will to live along a street in Lower Manhattan on a sultry night, in guises as various as a gay man whose bandanna in his left pocket tells you what he wants, or along Wall Street in a quick-stepping lawyer woman whose briefcase cuts through the crowd like a juggernaut. And we admire it.

You can see it on an evening in spring in young lovers who know what they want, and in old people who, in the city of New York, which I love, choose to fight their way through those muggy streets just to be out there where the action is, and leave the rockers to bury the dead.

You can see it on a perplexing canvas that you cannot understand but the passion of whose painter you can feel.

And you can hear it in a summer night's jazz.

We see it and we see ourselves, and we know this man whose consum-mate purposefulness sizes up his situation and does what he must to save his life. "Quick, write eighty! You, write fifty!" He goes for it.

And whatever we may think of his morality, Jesus was strangely indif-ferent to that. That is the very point at which some hearers of this parable inevitably hang up: "Why would Jesus commend a crook?" Whatever we think of his morality, something in us knows him and admires him.

The twenty-eight-year-old man complained, even whined, late into the night: "Parents, history, bad breaks, genes, whatever; I've been short-changed."

"Look," the pastor said, "if that's the way you see it, that life has given you a wooden leg, you had better learn to dance with it." Corny words, but they were the right words for him. They changed his life.

I don't have to tell you what it means to lose a job, or maybe I do. But plenty of people these days can tell you what it's like. At least for this manager it is his very life. "I cannot dig. I will not beg." And so he moves. We like his spunk, his cleverness, his action.

I went to see the burial place of Willa Cather up in Jaffrey Center, New Hampshire. It is located in a quiet church graveyard beside one of those beautiful, old picture-calendar Congregational churches. Cather wrote a wonderful story in Jaffrey Center, about a very purposeful priest in colonial New Mexico. About four gravestones down (if you're ever there, don't miss it!) is another grave, and it's marked "Lizzie. She done all she could."

I think we could easily end this story with verse 7 and leave our friend to his wits and his will to live. That would be enough for us to see as Jesus talks about what it is like to seize the kingdom of God. Our imagination could maybe even lead us into his future—that he would be so admired for his cleverness and his wit that, being fired, he would quickly have a place in the houses of those whom he has favored.

There's that whiz kid out in California who broke the code, invaded the corporate computer, learned how to use it so that he got AT&T to deliver one truckload after another of electronic equipment to him. What was it, a million dollars? And he ended up being hired by Ma Bell. Right?

In any case, we're with him, this clever, intrepid man who wants to go on living and does something about it.

It's what Saul Bellow shows us in *Henderson, the Rain King*, whose litany is always, "Man want to live, man want to live."

Jesus said the kingdom of God is like this. He saw more of the gracious reign of God among us, God's will for our life, in those who go for it—for this gift of life—than in those who too easily take the pink slip and go their way.

And we can understand, as much as we want health and wholeness for everybody, that Lutheran friend of mine who loves his pipe and ends most days with a scotch. His doctor told him, "You've got to give up both." He changed doctors.

It isn't hard for us to say to this shyster, "Good for you." In any case, Jesus said the kingdom of God is like that. If you want to know something about it, look at this man.

And yet, we want verse 8, too, and I think we must have it whether we want it or not. Kenneth Bailey, who has written a wonderful book on the parables called *Poet and Peasant*, says we must have verse 8. The master commends the steward for his cleverness. Bailey says that this is the end to a parabolic ballad; the ballad is not complete unless we come back to the servant meeting again with the master.[2] Somehow it just doesn't seem quite finished if he's not back in his office. As Bailey sees it, the stress is not only on the manager's determined cleverness, but on the master's mercy, as well. Grace is, as it were, the context of grab. It is that mercy by which we are always surrounded that makes it possible for us any day of the week, any time and place, in whatever way, to go for it.

Even as the story begins, we see a benevolent landowner, no doubt about it. He does not punish or imprison our friend; he could have done that. He simply calls him to hand over his ledgers and move out of the office. Very mild treatment! It is this graciousness, says Kenneth Bailey, on which the wily servant is finally counting. He is banking on it enough to run the risk he runs. His action in relieving the debtors of part of what is owed his master wins for his master favor in the village. What a great thing to do! What a nice guy! And it is this same graciousness upon which the servant presumes which saves his own future.

Make no mistake, this man is one of Jesus' dramatic rogues, along with the unmerciful servant, the lazy neighbor who pulls the covers over his head at midnight, the man who hides a treasure unearthed on another's land. Jesus seemed indifferent to the morality of his characters—as we count morality—so long as we could see them . . . identify with them. And we can.

The word for the manager's office is the Greek root of the word "economics," and it means the care of the house. And he has, apparently for private advantage, betrayed both his master and the common good. Apparently this estate is big enough that it is crucial to the economy of the whole region.

So maybe it would be better to leave it as Crossan would: an unmitigated story of cleverness, of a quick response to crisis. That is what Jesus wants us to see in this story—that the call to us is an ultimate call.

But we want to keep verse 8, and I think we must. Because we know that he, like us, both in private life and in the commonweal, will, in the days of good graces and in the final day of reckoning, be upheld finally not by his wits or his cleverness but by divine mercy.

For our part, we will strive and struggle. We will run the risk and seize the day and even as cities burn, the good die young, and children go hungry, we will still plant gardens and enjoy the summer, try to be for each other, and believe somehow deep down that you and I in our own time and place, preaching sermons, doing our work, have a part to play for peace and justice in God's economy. We will try, despite all, to seize the day, to take the time to squeeze it all out, to go for life and love. And then finally, in the midst of it, surrender, each of us, to the quality of mercy. Poignant moments of your life and mine are probably those in which we do a balancing act between realizing our own life, individually and with each other, and living toward what Jesus called eternity.

It's there in *E.T.* A wonderful movie, one you see twice. Steven Spielberg sets us up to be scared and terrorized by alien space invaders, only to show us some wonderful children and a fetus-like creature from outer space who is more human than we are. The children live through this with courage and abandon. Fight. Pedal those bikes like mad. And then, they have to trust the love which is between them and E.T. as he sails away. E.T. says, "Come." Elliot says, "Stay." Holding on, doing all that they can for each other, letting it be what it can be. But in the end, there's only the rainbow between them and the confidence that they are both part of something much bigger.

Or take a birthday party: presents, funny hats, cake with too much icing, all of which say quite simply, "I love you and I'm glad you were born." But you couldn't just come out and say it that way, could you? No. "I'll bake you a cake. I'll wear a funny hat." Candles numbered and wished over, celebrating and stalling time. And then finally amid limp balloons and crumbs, we find ourselves into another year and our wish a prayer, "Lamb of God have mercy on us, and give us another one." We who before this birthday is forgotten—long before another comes—will fail those we love.

Or take the Fourth of July. I've never had one that hit me so hard or so beautifully. Out in the country we were, by the lake, sun, breeze, thirty friends and more. Sounds of volleyball and water fights and an old-fashioned churning of ice cream, all of those sounds saying, "I love you." But you couldn't come out on the Fourth of July and say that. People drifting through a day wishing they were in Finland or someplace where the sun never goes down and it would keep on going . . . letting be, but, under it all, going for it.

"Let's take a walk. You thirsty? Come on in, the water's fine. I love you." Seizing the moment, the human moment. Still life of human joy on a sunny slope, everybody quiet. And there's the lump in your throat as you dish up the ice cream. You've been soaking raisins in rum for three days, and it becomes with each dip more than food.

Then it begins to end. You have given it all you've got. Everybody has, but it begins to end. Right in the middle of great saves at the net, picking wildflowers so vivid that they look like they'd never die but are wilting already as the daylilies close when the sun goes down, trying to hold on. We aim our sputtering rockets from twenty beer bottles out across the lake and set alight a bonfire that a friend started building the last fifth of July. The sun goes down, the fire flares and recedes. All the exuberance, joy, and hope of the day, then the fading of the fire flickering in our faces. People in the circle trying to hold on to the time—to each other—for dear life. When the fire goes to embers, and the faces fade into the dark, and the first car lights start down the lane, Wilfred finds a rake, and he starts like mad pulling the unburned logs into the fire, keeping it going.

Finally, despite all our giving and taking, and laughing and loving, it has to end in, "God have mercy on us. Lamb of God, grant us your peace."

You know of what I speak. You gather flowers, cook the food, pour the wine, as if everything in the world depended upon this moment and your part in it. And then in the middle of it, you know, and the greater the joy, the more you know that it will go.

It is in the face of the father who works as hard as he can and gives his best and reveals in the way that he looks at his wife and his children even as they are driving down the road, neither Metropolitan Life nor I can give you all I want you to have.

It was in that man at the gas station the day when Richard, that tired man, trying to fix our busted hose and get us on over here so I could preach a sermon—sunburned face, wind-damaged skin, pouring water in two steaming cars—with that look on his face as he said, "I will do all I can for you." Then his last word to us was, "Well, I guess it's time to go home."

It was there yesterday in Philadelphia, as we looked at the paintings of Thomas Eakins. The strong, lithe bodies of rowers on the Schuylkill, their backs bent to the oars; beautiful women of Victorian Philadelphia; the surgeons at their work, and on every face that sideward, downward, longing look that Eakins paints so well: that edge of sadness, that seeing through. "Lord, have mercy on us." We can only go so far.

It is there in Saint Cross cemetery, Oxford, where Charles Williams is buried. Williams's play *Grab and Grace* reflects the struggles of his own life. His gravestone bears the epitaph "Under the Mercy."

So I want to keep John Crossan and Kenneth Bailey on this parable, to take the easy way out. How could we stop with verse 7, or jump to verse 8? Better to keep them both. This wily man who acts as if everything, everything, his very life, depends upon what he does now. And the one who knows finally, in the end, that at the depths, in the very midst of seizing the day, we are held and saved at last, every last one of us, in the eternal mercy of God revealed to us in Jesus Christ our Lord.

ENJOYING WHAT BELONGS TO GOD
I Corinthians 16:1–4

James E. Mead

On a recent mission trip to India, I learned about a fascinating practice of the Evangelical Church of India. When the church baptizes a new believer, this new member of Christ's church is given the gift of a coconut palm tree. The new believer takes it home and plants it, and within four years, this tree starts to bear fruit. When the coconut palm is young, it will bear about fifty dollars' worth of coconuts a year, and, when it matures, it will provide about one hundred dollars of annual income. In India, one hundred dollars of yearly income is a significant amount of money, even for the middle class.

The church gives new believers coconut palms for two reasons. First, almost everyone in India is needy, and the income helps to provide for their needs. Second, the coconut palms teach a lesson about Christian stewardship. The church tells each new believer that it expects them to give 10 percent, a tithe, of whatever income they get out of that coconut palm tree.

The "coconut tree plan" is a wonderful idea and a great expression of the deeper meanings of Christian stewardship. The income the family gets from the tree comes free, entirely as a gift. They don't buy the tree; it is given to them. Also, the tithe, the 10 percent, is money they get free. The family is able to enjoy the fruits of a gift given freely to them and also to have the joy of freely giving something away themselves.

Moreover, these new Christians play a crucial role as stewards in all of this. They have a choice. If they wish, they can take the tree home, throw it in a corner, and let it die, never growing any coconuts. But they also can choose to plant their tree in a good spot, take care of it, watch over it, and harvest the coconuts. Everything depends on their decision making. No one forces them to tithe. There are no "coconut tree tithing police" to make sure they are giving 10 percent of the coconut income to the Lord's work. People are free to choose to give or not.

The idea that human possessions are really gifts comes from the Bible. The biblical understanding of wealth and possessions is that everything comes from God and everything belongs to God. Nothing actually belongs to us; rather, as Psalm 24 puts it clearly, "The earth is the LORD's and all that is in it, the world, and those who live in it." Everything and everybody belongs to God. "If I were hungry," God says to the people, "I would not tell you, for the world and all that is in it is mine" (Ps. 50:12).

Sometimes it is difficult to remember that God really owns everything, because you and I work hard for our incomes. We have sweated over our jobs and focused energy on our careers and on making our net worth grow. Some of us have been through tough job negotiations, even gone on strike to improve our working conditions. We have toiled for what we have. But the truth is that we came into the world with nothing, and we will leave with nothing. We will live sixty, eighty, maybe a hundred years, but when we die everything we have accumulated and everything we think is ours will stop being ours and will pass on to somebody else. A hundred years is a long time, but in the great span of time, even a hundred years is hardly anything. For a few fleeting moments, we have possession of a few things, but they belonged to somebody else before us, and they will belong to others after us.

The air we breathe, the water we drink, the wonder of life itself, the planet we live on, the universe—we brought none of these things into being. They are gifts we enjoy out of the overflow of God's love. The love of God, the gift of Jesus Christ, forgiveness of our sins, the call into Christian community, the comfort of the Holy Spirit, eternal life—none came from us, each is a gift to us from God.

To remember that God owns everything prompts a remarkable shift in our view of stewardship. Usually when we think of stewardship (of giving to charitable causes, if you want), we define it as our giving to God or to the church something that belongs to us. But in the Bible, stewardship is just the reverse—our freely using, enjoying, and giving what already belongs to God.

Last year, the sixth-grade Sunday school class in my church learned this truth about stewardship. Each child in the class was given a bunch of stickers that read, "This belongs to Jesus." They were instructed to put these little stickers on everything at home they owned—compact disks, roller blades, bicycles, everything—to remind them that all of these things actually belong to Jesus and to encourage them to use these things in ways pleasing to Jesus. They should have given me a whole batch of those little stickers. I would have put a little sticker on my stereo speakers that I love so much. These speakers belong to Jesus. This car and this savings account belong to Jesus. I could put one on my calendar to show me that this time belongs to Jesus. Everything ultimately belongs to God. It isn't the other way around at all. We only think it is.

Looking at the world in this new way takes some doing, some significant changing in the way we think about possessions, in how we use money, and in our behavior. God gives us everything, and God also calls us to give a portion of that away, to pass it along to others. Do you believe this? If so, what portion would that be? The scripture calls us to give a tithe, 10 percent.

Now, how do we get to the place where we are giving, as Paul guides us to understand in 1 Corinthians 16, regularly, proportionately, and faithfully? How do families get to the place where they are tithing? Some people are very fortunate and blessed. They grew up in homes where tithing was taught from the time they were small. But for most of us, we have to learn tithing on our own and grow into it.

It was that way for William Diehl. Diehl is the author of several books, including *The Monday Connection,* in which he tells the story of his family's growth in stewardship. He was the manager of sales for Bethlehem Steel for thirty-two years, in a very responsible position rewarded with a fine income. But when Diehl and his wife, Judy, were first challenged to tithe, they were absolutely overwhelmed by the idea. Two members of their little church in Detroit came to them and talked with them about tithing. The idea seemed completely impossible to the Diehls, as it might seem to many of us. At the time, the Diehls were giving only 2 percent of their income away.

But the two visitors showed them how they could get started. They were to begin where they were. Who can start anywhere else? So William and Judy started at 2 percent, and every time William was given a raise, they increased their giving by 1 percent. In a few years, they were giving 10 percent, and, by that time, it fit comfortably into their budget. Then, they moved from 10 percent of their "take home" income to 10 percent of their total income. Later they began to tithe their investment dividends and interest income as well.

Judy and William found that one of the most meaningful parts of their stewardship program was deciding what to do with all this money that they were passing on in God's name. The whole family would participate in the choices, sometimes deciding to send the money directly to people they knew were in need or to programs to assist the needy. Through this, one of the daughters became interested in helping orphans in Asia and eventually adopted an orphan through a relief ministry.

What about us? God does not need our money. We need to give. We have received bountifully from God, and it is good for us to give. It's a way of saying thank you to God for all we've received. It's a way of acknowledging the One who ultimately owns everything. It's a way of getting the right perspective, and the best reminder I know of this truth that everything we have really belongs to God is either tithing or working out a plan to get to the place where we are tithing.

I encourage you this week to do three things to come to grips with your own giving. The first is to set some short-term goals for your giving. What will you give in the next year? Set a percentage. Talk with God about this, and talk about it as a family, including your children.

Second, I encourage you to set a long-term goal. What level of giving do you want to reach in the next five years? Many set the tithe as their goal. Others target 20 percent of their income, or more. What is God calling you to do?

Third, develop a concrete plan for meeting your short-term and long-term goals. Nobody gets there all at once. Plan what you will buy and not buy, what you will do and not do, how you will steward God's resources— the things that God has given you to enjoy, to pass along, and to enjoy passing along. What will you do to increase your giving in the long run? How will you go about that? William and Judy Diehl increased their giving 1 percent every time he got a raise. Other people have increased their giving 1 percent per year until they reached their goal. What will be your plan?

In my own family, it has been important to us to know what our goals are and to work together to realize them with God's help. We haven't always been in complete agreement about this. We've had concerns about it, even arguments at times. We haven't always met our goals, and we haven't always been proud of our giving either. But the planning, the discussion, the decisions—all the struggles over the question of good stewardship have changed our attitude about our own money and set us more free in dealing with money and everything that we own.

In the meantime, the Lord is with us as we think about all that God has given us to enjoy and all that we can enjoy passing along in God's name to other people.

TAMPER WITH EVIDENCE
Matthew 22:15–22

William R. Leety

One day, the religious leaders sent their disciples to Jesus, and they said, "Teacher, we know that you are sincere and teach the way of God in accordance with truth, and show deference to no one; for you do not regard people with partiality"—which means, "Smile, God loves you, but don't take it personally." They continued, "Tell us, then, what you think. Is it lawful to pay taxes to the emperor or not?" In other words, what should we do with our money? Should we support a tax levy for city schools? Should we support tax funds for children's services? For mental health and alcohol rehab services? Should we vote for casinos and roll the dice on public education?

Jesus said, "Show me the coin used for the tax." When they brought him a coin, he asked, "Whose head is this, and whose title?"

"The emperor's," they answered.

Then Jesus said, "Give therefore to the emperor the things that are the emperor's, and to God the things that are God's." When they heard this, they were amazed.

But what did Jesus mean? How do we know what belongs to God and what belongs to the emperor? Is education of God, of the emperor, or of the casino? What about programs for children? How do we decide? And we may as well be blunt. As Joan Rivers says, "Can we talk?" What about what we give to the church? Is the church of God or is it of the emperor? How do we know? These are important questions, because Jesus says we should give to the emperor and to God what belongs to each.

Let's look again at the story. The Pharisees and Herodians come to Jesus, and they begin the dialogue with the kind of blarney that often precedes a question in that culture: "Teacher, we know that you are sincere, and teach the way of God in accordance with truth, and show deference to no one; for you do not regard people with partiality." This is merely a ceremonial warm-up, something like a member of Congress saying, "My distinguished colleague from the great state of Ohio." It is ironic, of course, that the Pharisees unknowingly speak the truth: Jesus does embody truth, does teach the way, is sincere, and is "no respecter of persons."

Then ceremony yields to trickery as the religious leaders ask, "So, teacher, shall we pay taxes to the emperor, who claims to be a god, or should we not?" Everyone knows that any public political question about tax, about money, is a good trap, but in Jesus' day the issue of tax money was particularly sensitive. Even the coins themselves were red flags because Caesar's bust was on every coin, constantly reminding Jews that Judah was a Roman colony. Every time they exchanged money, Jews held in their hands the shameful evidence that their people were colonized, not free, and that their God could not, or would not, overthrow Caesar.

"Whose head is this?" Jesus asks, holding a coin.

"The emperor's." They all knew the answer, and they all knew the implications. But what is really at stake isn't the image on the coin; it's the image on your heart. It's not that the emperor gets into your pocket; it's that the emperor gets into your head, into your soul.

"Give to the emperor the things that belong to the emperor." That is what Jesus says, but it's tricky, isn't it? Ohio State football now wears the image of the Nike swoosh. So are the Buckeyes of Ohio State University or of Nike? If players ran faster in Reeboks, could the universities, would the universities return the coins marked with the swoosh and wear Reebok shoes and jerseys? How far can one go and not lose something essential?

Political campaign financing raises the same questions. So Philip Morris and Arthur Daniels Midland get into the Republicans' pockets, or the United Auto Workers and international business folk get into the Democrats'—no big deal, we are just talking about pockets and this is politics as usual, we say. But what if it's more than just pockets? What if these contributors, or the AARP, the American Medical Association, or, for that matter, the Presbyterian church get into one's soul? If the emperor puts the emperor's mark on your soul, and most of us think it's a short route from pocket to soul, then you're not free. Give Liggett and Myers what belongs to Liggett and Myers, give the National Rifle Association what belongs to the NRA, but don't give the conscience, which belongs to God, to the NRA.

Whose face is on the coin? Whose initials? What belongs to the emperor? What belongs to God? The real question is not about surfaces but about depths. The real question is not whose inscription is on the coin but whose inscription is on us? The real question is not whether the coin belongs to the emperor but how much of us belongs to the emperor and how much of us belongs to God? Underneath Jesus' saying is the biblical story of creation; there it is said of human beings that they were made "in the image of God, God created them, male and female." At creation, the Pharisees and Herodians and the emperor and Jesus and you and I are marked with God's initials. We're signed sculptures! In baptism, we are marked by the cross on our forehead. The issue is not who owns the coin but who owns the person. And, after sometimes years of deciding to whom we belong, we give ourselves to whom we belong.

I see children leave their own homes to look after their older parents. I see these children spend their days, even their years, caring for these people. If we ask them why they make such sacrifices for their parents, they will say, "I belong to them in love."

I see a woman take a second job to pay for a child's college tuition. Why? "I belong to them in love."

Why does a scholar, published for the first time, give all proceeds from the sale of the book to the university where she works? "I'm thankful for the nurturing and support. I belong to the university."

We give ourselves according to our love, so when Jesus says, "Give to God the things that are God's," this is about love, not obligation. In baptism, each of us is marked as loved by God. Remember when God's hand covered Moses, leaving God's fingerprints all over Moses? The generous God leaves a mark on each to show we belong to God. But we tamper with that evidence of God's passing close to us. We smudge the print. We bear God's likeness on our bodies, God's inscription in our baptism. "Give to God what is God's."

I knew an eye surgeon who went to a mission hospital and performed sight-saving surgeries: thirteen thousand a year, forty a day, for thirty-three years. He knows to whom he belongs.

Stewardship Sunday is not just about a pledge to the church. If you don't believe the church is of God, you shouldn't give. Stewardship Sunday is a symbol that means giving ourselves. We have been marked with love and grace and mercy and generosity by God. Give your money and time and energy, give them in love. Don't give them away; give them to the God to whom you belong.

So, how much of you belongs to the emperor, or to the company? Oh yes, sometimes the emperor and the company do the work of God. If they didn't, we wouldn't have anything to do with them. What we offer here on Sunday is a symbol of what we offer through the week. Our offering on Sunday is a rehearsal, a practicing of the act of giving ourselves in preparation for our giving Monday through Saturday. Out in the world we still bear the image of God, and we don't tamper with the evidence. Here we give to God what is God's . . . and there too.

STRAIGHT TALK
AND STEWARDSHIP
Matthew 22:15–22

George Chorba

Several years ago, the British writer and lecturer C. S. Lewis, asked to speak on the subject of Christian stewardship, began with these words: "On the whole, God's love for us is a much safer subject to think about than our love for Him." I feel very much that way myself. Sometimes it is much easier, and safer really, just to skirt the whole subject of stewardship, of how we give shape and substance to our love for God.

But there is another side to that coin. A young Scot once told his pastor, "I'm fed up with the church and Christianity. All I ever hear is 'Give, give, give!'" The pastor, Donald Ross, fixed his steel blue eyes on the man, and in his soft Inverness accent replied, "Well, can you think of a better definition of Christianity than that?" Give, give, give!

We may choose to skirt the subject entirely, but the fact remains that stewardship is the way we define our faith and make it personal. During stewardship season in our congregation a special brochure was sent to every home. On the last page, there was a photograph of a dozen or so children from the kindergarten church school class, along with a caption that read, "Working for the Future." Children . . . the future, the connection was obvious; everybody knows that our children represent the future of the church.

But there was something unusual about that photograph. The children were pictured standing together at the entrance to the church, facing into the sun. Their eyes squinted slightly so that there was the hint of a quizzical look on their faces. One of the smallest of them was a child who looked out from behind long bangs, and a finger touched the corner of her mouth. It was as if she and the others were waiting for an answer to a question they had not yet heard.

Well, we are about to raise that question with each other now. The question is this: What is the gift you and I are prepared to give in the year ahead? In another place in that brochure, amid pictures of the church family, was this simple and straightforward expression of the gospel: "We are the church because we care about the good news of Jesus Christ. . . . Our love should not be mere words and empty talk; it must be true love which shows itself in action." For each of us, stewardship is what we do after we have said what we believe. Generation after generation of Christians before us have put their love into action in order that we might have a future in the church. They have passed this legacy to us. Now it is our turn. Our actions are part of the unfolding of God's love in this place. The question those children are asking is, "What is the gift you and I are prepared to give in the year ahead? What gift are we willing to give that our children might have a future in the church?"

Before we try to answer that question, let us go again to the biblical text. In this story in Matthew, the Pharisees and Herodians tried to entangle Jesus with some cleverly worded questions about money. "Tell us," they said, "how we are to use this money?" And they knew, of course, that whatever he said, they could find fault with it one way or another. But he simply took a coin in his hand, examined it, and said, "Render to Caesar the things that are Caesar's, and to God the things that are God's!"

What are "the things that are God's?" Those words of Jesus have often been misconstrued to imply that some things belong to God and some do not and that there is, for each of us, a kind of divine tariff levied upon all of our resources. In this view, each of us has a duty to come across, to parcel out our possessions and to give God his due portion.

I want to challenge this thinking of God as some kind of celestial bookkeeper whose only interest in life is the return on an investment. That isn't what the story in Matthew says at all. What are the things that are God's? If we are to tell the truth, our whole life is God's, not simply some part of our life but all of who and what we are. Stewardship is not narrowly and exclusively about what we possess; it is about our relation to the God who possesses us. Stewardship is about our whole life.

Here is a story that is apocryphal but, at the same time, full of truth. Jesus, it seems, returned to heaven, and, inevitably as such stories go, was greeted by one of the heavenly gatekeepers. He asked Jesus what provisions he had made for perpetuating the work he had started on earth.

"Well, I chose twelve men and spent three years with them, training them, motivating them, and challenging them to be my representatives to the farthest corners of the earth," Jesus said.

"What kind of men are they?" the questioner asked.

"Ordinary men, fishermen, tax collectors, farmers, workers, and, oh, yes, one doctor," was Jesus' response.

"And what tools did you give them to work with?"

"Their tools," Jesus said, "are their minds, their spirits, their souls . . . in other words, their entire beings and whole selves . . . and whatever they can produce and develop."

"And what if they fail? What other plan do you have?"

"I have no other plan. If they fail, then my mission fails," Jesus said. "But they will not fail."

Our Lord left his work in the keeping of human hands, human minds, human hearts. If we fail, he fails, his work fails. But we will not fail. We will not fail because failure is a judgment we make and not one that God makes. "I know the plans I have for you," says the Lord, "plans for good and not for evil, to give you a future and a hope." And then in the New Testament: "And I am sure that he who began a good work in you will bring it to completion."

I have that same confidence about the future, about our future. We will not fail. And that is not simply religious rhetoric. Obviously we do fail. We fail in many things. What is it about us, though, that will not fail? It is the witness of your life that will not fail, because that is what will live beyond you, beyond all the other successes and failures you can tally in a lifetime. It is the witness of your life that will not fail.

Henry B. Wright has written a great deal about the church, and in one of his recent books he says, "Preachers can talk themselves blue in the face, but the living witness of a single parishioner can accomplish in one minute what they have been talking about for years. Call to your pulpits ever-so-eloquent preachers with ever-so-steely hair and ever-so-silvery tongues and ever-so-golden hearts; the lay person's life is still the decisive witness in this world. The pew is the pulpit that finally counts."

I believe that. Your life, and the pew where you sit, is the pulpit that counts in this church, because stewardship is what we do after we have said what we believe.

The most important witness of our life together is what you and I are willing to build for the future. That requires time and imagination. It requires prayer and focused concentration. It requires energy and imagination. It also requires money. And in that regard, our church is the inheritor of a legacy far more important than any endowment account we might ever have. And the legacy is this: It is a legacy from history, and from a long history of being the church from the time of the Protestant Reformation.

For prior to that time, during the Middle Ages, people's wealth was most commonly used for personal adornment, for grand houses, and for conspicuous and extravagant display. John Calvin, however, taught that money, just like life itself, was a blessing from God, a blessing entrusted to his children for his use and glory. No longer was money considered sterile and barren, as it had been before the Reformation. Now it was regarded as dynamic, as a tool for active use in the service of God and of all humanity.

Today, there are nearly two billion people in the world who wear the name that, for us, is above every name, the name of Christ. That is more Christians than the world has ever had before. But there are about twice as many who are not Christians in the world today. And that, too, is more than ever before. Those nearly four billion men and women and children of promise are our challenge and opportunity today.

In our own country, and I know it is true for the communities we are able to serve, only slightly more than one in three people are ever reached and touched by the churches today. That is our challenge and our opportunity, as well; to grow both spiritually and in the scope of our witness and involvement with people who are our friends, but who often live lives of anonymous faith. Our mandate is the same as it was for the Twelve. We are still to go into the world and share good news with people, to preach and teach and make disciples and baptize. And the great thing about this great commission is that Jesus told us what to do . . . but not how to do it. The what, he was clear about . . . the how, he has left in our hands . . . and to our own ingenuity.

That is our challenge and our opportunity!

R.S.V.P.
Matthew 22:34–40

Carol Ann Fleming

One of the highlights of my day is going to the mailbox. When I was a child, that meant a long walk up the steep driveway, or the occasional treat of getting a ride up and back from my father on the lawn mower. In one little town where we once lived, it meant taking the whole family on an excursion around the corner to the local post office and meeting half the town for a quick chat about the weather. Here, it means just a short ten yards to retrieve what usually amounts to a lot of useless catalogues and junk mail for past residents. Still, there is that moment of anticipation of what will be in the mail—perhaps an unexpected windfall, a letter from a family member or a friend.

Sometimes the mail brings an invitation to come to a celebration—a birthday party or a wedding. At the bottom of these invitations there is often a small notation to R.S.V.P., *répondez, si'l vous plaît,* respond, if you please. In your mailboxes this week you also received an invitation, an invitation from this church to increase your stewardship pledge to spread the mission and ministry God is accomplishing through this congregation. I hope your response to that invitation is one of celebration, rather than begrudging one more request for money. But I do want you to know that this invitation comes with a request to R.S.V.P. We can R.S.V.P. as we experience God's love and share our resources, and, in the case of our church, R.S.V.P. means not only "respond, if you please" but also some other important insights.

The "R," for starters, represents the Reformed tradition, in which we stand and which shaped our faith community. Our ancestors in the sixteenth century were not trying to revolt against the church but to reform it, to recall it to the faith of the early church. They stressed continuity to the creeds of the early church. They set faithfulness to scripture as the measure of church life. What they sought was not a new faith but a reclamation of the Word of God. The Reformation also stressed the catholicity of the church, the one united church of which Jesus Christ alone was head and Lord.

The rallying cry of the Reformers was *salvatio gratia*, salvation by grace alone, and salvation by grace is the "S" in R.S.V.P. The good news of God's amazing love is this, that while we were yet sinners Christ died for us. We have a personal relationship with our savior that we do not merit or even ask for. Jesus freely gave this life for me and for each of you. Because we did not earn our salvation, because it was the freely given gift of God's love for us, we are freed from the burden of our sins and are free to respond from love rather than guilt or fear. Grace is God's personal relationship to us. God's relationship is not dependent on what we offer to God, but on God's willingness to offer everything to us. The God who acted for us in the past is the God who will act on our behalf in the future. Faith believes that in all things God works together for good in those who love the Lord. As Luther said, "Faith is a lively, reckless confidence in the grace of God."

The pastor of a church in New York told me they have three questions they ask about everything they do as a church. First, is Christ the reason and the center of this ministry? Second, is this ministry necessary for the neighboring community? And, third, is our vision of ministry in this project large enough? They don't believe that God, who parted the Red Sea, who moves mountains, and who moves hard hearts, works in small ways. This church went from fifty members to five hundred in ten years and is in the process of building a million-dollar community center. This is a congregation with a "lively, reckless confidence in the grace of God."

The "V" represents our vocation. Each of us has been called by God into special service. This is not to say that each of us should be clergy but that every Christian is a minister for Christ. Today, the term vocation has become degraded to a mere description of how we earn a living, but originally it meant the larger calling of a Christian to be a Christian, a calling to be part of the work of God in every activity of life—a vocation from which there is no vacation. The Reformers abolished the difference between sacred and secular callings. For them, there was a unity to life and God could be served equally well any place within the whole. To love God and neighbor meant to strive for justice in the workplace. If we are indeed serving Christ in our work as well as in our worship, we will begin to examine the way we do business.

Finally, "P" stands for proclamation, the most important part of our response to God's invitation. Proclamation is not just preaching, but a life that communicates the joy of God's grace, a life lived in praise, a life, as Paul says, marked by courage, gentleness, affection, self-giving.

There is a spirit of celebration in this body of Christ. We have good news to share! God has issued a personal invitation to each one of you—how will you R.S.V.P.?

PERSONAL PREPARATION
FOR STEWARDSHIP

THE HOUSE THAT LOVE BUILDS
2 Corinthians 4:16–5:10

Wanda Sevey

Once when I was a child, I discovered a loose sweet potato in the bottom of the kitchen vegetable drawer. With a third-grader's determination, I decided to try to recreate the science experiment we had done in school earlier that fall. Using a chair, I climbed into the cupboard and found the box of toothpicks. An hour later, surrounded by broken toothpicks, the project was ready. The sweet potato was balanced precariously in a glass of water, held up by the toothpicks. The goal of the project was to see the potato take root in the water. I had seen potatoes growing in my grandfather's garden, so I was familiar with the leaves of the plant. What amazed me was being able to see, through the glass, the roots visible and growing. The intricate system of big thick roots, with smaller roots branching off, and small feathers of roots in the water was beautiful and mysterious.

When I think about giving money to God, I find myself thinking more and more about what's underneath the surface of our giving. I think about the root of stewardship and the meaning of stewardship in our life together here at church. Last summer, I identified one feathery root of stewardship when I went to visit my three-year-old nephew, Jon. Jon was in no mood for a visit that August evening. I had dropped by after dinner to spend time with my sister and her family. Jon had just finished his first-ever week of Vacation Bible School, topped off by an afternoon swim party at a friend's pool. He had missed his nap that afternoon, too. He was exhausted. "I need to go to bed," he said to his mom. Mom didn't act quickly enough and soon he was clenching his blanket with one fist and angrily shaking the other. "I need to go to bed now!" He cried all the way up the stairs to his bedroom. My sister followed him up the stairs, comforted him, tucked him in, and stood beside his bed until he felt calm and safe. A friend of mine says, "Sometimes, don't you wish you were still small enough to be carried up the stairs in your parents' arms and tucked into bed?"

Watching Jon reminded me that, whether you are three years old or thirty or seventy, life can be tough. Life has its share of exhaustion, worry, trials, and disappointments. Life can wear on us. Beyond the regular routine, life as Christ's followers can be not only tiring but also dangerous. Paul says he suffered shipwreck, arrest, beatings, and imprisonment. No wonder he says, "Outwardly we are wasting away." Just as the pounding ocean waves can wear rocks to sand or a steady, insistent drip can carve caves in mountains, sometimes we can feel as if we are being worn down until it seems we have no option but to angrily shake our fist and withdraw from the world.

And yet, that's not the whole picture. Paul says that while our outer lives face wear and tear, spiritually we can be safe and secure. At a high school graduation ceremony last spring, Attorney General Janet Reno said that, when she was a girl, her mother looked around one day at her life. She saw her growing family. She saw their tiny home. She saw her husband working from dawn to night to earn enough money to support his family. She knew they couldn't afford a larger house. She also knew they needed one. So she decided to build a new house herself. First, she went to the library and checked out books about new home construction. After she had read and studied them, she made appointments with contractors, visited them on work sites, and asked questions. Then she began to dig the foundation. She built that house with her own hands. She didn't cut corners. She studied the codes, and she built it to code. Years later, after her children were grown and her husband had died, the Southeastern part of the country was hit by a major hurricane. Storms battered the coastline from Florida to New Jersey. Houses and other buildings blew away like pup tents. But inside her sturdy home, Mrs. Reno waited out the storm by lighting a candle, sitting at her kitchen table, and reading her Bible.

God has built such a house for us through Christ. The death and resurrection of Christ creates a new reality, a new creation, a new home for us. It is a reality and a home not built by human hands but by the love and power of God in Christ. Because this house of Christ's love is built by God, it is eternal and cannot be destroyed. The storms can rage, our outer lives can be worn down. God does not promise we will be spared the storms and circumstances of life. In the storms of life, however, God does give us the strong house of Christ's love and presence to protect us. As Paul says, "Outwardly we are wasting away but inwardly we are being renewed day by day . . . we know that if this earthly tent is destroyed, we have a building from God, an eternal house in heaven."

Our outer lives may face storm and circumstance, but inside the house of Christ's love our lives can be secure. Not that the storms of life aren't real. Real storms do have real power to wreak havoc. Yet we proclaim that even in the midst of the storm, even in dangerous situations, there is a safety and a confidence that go deeper than circumstance and are rooted in God's promise to hold on to us and be with us.

I first thought about living in a house built by God years ago when I attended a church conference. I don't even remember the type of conference or why I was there, but I do remember a man telling me the story of the house he and his wife owned. When their last child graduated from high school and moved out of the house, they looked at their home and saw the wear and tear and all the marks that only years of raising children can place on a home. They decided that they would replace the sofa with the broken arm, paint over the fingerprints on the walls, and even add a sunporch. After receiving several bids from contractors, they sat down and looked at the numbers. The total was more than they expected but not more than they could afford. They would finally have the house they always wanted, except the more they thought about it, the less comfortable they became. They were Christians and faithful church members, and the more they looked at the bottom line the more they realized all the other things they could do with this money. Finally they made their decision. They gave the money to a recent refugee from Vietnam so that he could go to college. "We had always invested in ourselves, in our family, in our security, and in our comfort," said the man. "We decided to invest in the work of Christ and help someone else. We consider it one of our better investments."

The invitation to make an investment in a home built by God is available to all of us. But we are the ones who decide whether or not we want to actually move into this house God has built for us. It is not a house built with wood and nails; it is not a house you can see in a physical sense; we live in this house of God's love by faith. The only way to live in the house of God's presence is to move into it by faith. That kind of move can be frightening.

When I was an assistant director at a church camp, the outdoor adventure supervisor decided to take the staff on a Saturday rappeling trip. He drove us in the camp van to the vertical face of a rock that was about thirty feet high. "It's easy. Just trust the rope!" he'd say with confidence as he strapped the equipment on each of us. The only problem was that in order to trust the rope—in order to discover that it was trustworthy—you had to stand on the very edge of the cliff, turn your back to the abyss and walk backward over the edge. Only when you were over the edge did you discover that the rope was actually going to hold you. Then you had to push off from the rock and rappel down to solid ground. That first step off the back of the rock was the most difficult. In fact, I couldn't make it. I had all the equipment on. I walked to the edge of the cliff. I looked over. I backed away, took off the equipment, and walked back down the trail.

The only way to discover that the house of God's love is trustworthy is to walk through the door by faith. The only way to discover that Christ's love and presence will keep you safe is to anchor yourself in him while the winds of the storm rush like a freight train past your door. That's when you discover that you're in one piece; you're safe.

That is one of the roots of stewardship. Living safely in the house of Christ's love is the source of courageous and bold lives. Come the power of storms or the power of hell, we live in Christ and do the work he has called us to do. Just last week the officers of a nearby congregation were trying to decide whether or not to become a host church for the Interfaith Hospitality Network. It would mean housing homeless families in their church several weeks a year, providing hospitality, meals, and a safe place for families to be together. They had a bit of trouble making this decision. There were fears and questions: "What if we fail? What if the neighbors disapprove? What if we find out we can't get enough people to help?"

They were almost ready to decide against the project when one of the elders said, "If we only do the things we are certain won't fail, then we aren't living by faith. Stepping out in faith means risking. It means doing what Christ is calling us to do, whether it's scary or not." The motion passed. They had made a decision against living in fear and for living in the house of Christ's love.

This is the beginning of Stewardship Emphasis here at this church. The church needs money to pay the bills. The church budget needs your gifts of money and skills if we are to have a ministry together. But stewardship is not rooted in money. It is rooted in our desire to walk by faith. Stewardship takes root when you walk into the house of God's love and decide to make your home there. Stewardship doesn't begin with money. It begins when we decide as individuals and as a church to give thanks to God for loving us, for sending Christ to be our home. Once we make that commitment, our home in Christ gives us the confidence and security to be generous givers in every way.

THE HEART OF THE MATTER: A LENTEN STEWARDSHIP SERMON
Jeremiah 31:31–34

Terry L. Chapman

Someone stopped me before worship this morning, after she had read the sermon title in the bulletin: "A Lenten Stewardship Sermon." "What's a stewardship sermon doing here in Lent?" she asked. "This is the middle of March. I thought stewardship was for November."

True, we are accustomed to hearing about stewardship during the fall annual emphasis. That's when we look toward the coming year, toward the budget, toward our financial commitments. Yet all of us know that true stewardship involves living faithfully and responsibly every month of the year. So maybe Lent is a good time to rediscover that stewardship is a way of life, not a season. Maybe Lent is a good time to move past all the trappings of the fall stewardship program, past the flip charts and overhead projections, beyond the pledge cards and the budget meetings. Necessary as they may be, they are not the most important thing; they are not the heart of the matter.

What is the heart of the matter? Well, maybe Lent is the best time to find out. Maybe Lent is the best time to peel back the covering from our acts of charity to see what lies underneath them all, to see, as the prophet Jeremiah put it, what is written on our hearts. Maybe of all the seasons in the church year, Lent is the best time to do this deep searching because it is the "low pressure zone" of the Christian year. The disturbing storms of Holy Week, the storms that threaten the very landscape of the human-divine relationship, are brewing. The wind is picking up, the menacing clouds are gathering, trouble is in the air, and now is the time we need to look at the heart. In this Lenten season of self-reflection and soul-searching, we can hear

Jeremiah speaking of a new covenant between God and people: "I will write it on their hearts; and I will be their God, and they shall be my people."

Jeremiah spoke these words to a people exiled in Babylon. Uprooted, enslaved, degraded, dehumanized, they felt, no doubt, that they had been abandoned by God. Perhaps we have not had the experience of being a refugee or captive in a foreign land, but we know something about the experience of God's absence. There are moments when prayers don't seem to come, when faith is compromised by doubt, when disappointment diminishes any sense of God's presence.

Jacques Ellul describes our own exile when he says that we turn on the evening news, and "a hundred disjointed and unpredictable happenings" are thrown into our homes.[1] We wonder: where is God in the random acts of violence that plague our world, in the betrayal of a loved one, in the grinding stress, in the deadly disease? Is God here, or is God absent? Where is God in a world that is "incomprehensible, touchy, disquieting as ghost's veils, a broken world, full of holes and full of the irrational."[2] Where is God in the times of exile? "There's a rare quality of silence surrounding certain atrocities," writes Elull, "an end-of-the-world silence . . . one has the impression that a presence has been withdrawn which could one day fill everything. That total absence of charity takes the form of the low-pressure area which brings storms."[3]

In this "low pressure" zone of human existence, when the silence of our own humanity is deafening and all of our resources do not seem to be enough to bring light into our darkness, there can be a new vulnerability of heart, and Lent is the "low pressure zone" of the Christian year, the time we need to look at the heart.

In the ancient world, the heart was considered the center of human life. The heart was the site of all thought, planning, reflection, explanation, and ambition. It was the place where the whole person experienced or suffered the full weight of joy, sorrow, anxiety, fear, and hope.[4] Even today, the heart still symbolizes the deepest and most authentic part of our being. It is in our hearts that we most deeply meet God, in the hidden depths of our being, at the center of who we are and all we have in us to become.

So what is the heart of the matter? If stewardship is a way of life, what kind of heart does it take?

First, it takes a heart that is quiet and still, a heart attentive to the possibility of God breaking into our busy lives, a heart that waits for an elusive Lord to comfort and direct us. I don't recall getting any direct help in seminary about how to listen for the guidance of the Spirit. More time was given to filling the head with information than to training the heart to be attentive and open to God. But knowing about God only in our heads is not sufficient for a deep and growing faith. For John Calvin, faith is "a firm and certain knowledge of God's benevolence toward us . . . both revealed in our minds and sealed upon our hearts through the Holy Spirit."

More and more people are beginning to discover the importance of creating space in their lives to grow still and attentive. Our days are busy. Moments fly by with alarming speed. Schedules are cluttered with things to do, books to read, jobs to be accomplished, deadlines to be met. Our lives are bombarded with minute-by-minute news coverage of world crises and local skirmishes. We are so skilled at doing that many of us have simply forgotten how to be. In fact, we have become a people who do not know how to define ourselves except by what we do, "I'm the CEO of XYZ," or by what we possess, "My other car is a Mercedes." We have forgotten who we really are at heart!

But, as Jeremiah reminds us, God promises, "I will write what really counts, what is most real, on my people's hearts; and I will be their God, and they shall belong to me." A person whose heart is still and attentive will be able to feel the movement of God's finger as these words are written upon it, "I am your God, and you are my child."

Second, it takes a heart of surrender. Indeed, attentiveness to God and stillness at the core of our being can only lead to a heart of surrender. There, in that "low pressure zone" of vulnerability and receptiveness, we are found by God, even in our exile, and we discover our true humanity. Our deepest desires, our greatest longings, our most authentic joys are not captured by us but captured for us, given to us as gifts in the loving words that God has inscribed upon our hearts. The heart of the matter is not seizing but surrendering.

However, surrendering is not easy to do. Most of us would rather be in charge than surrender. That's the appeal of the normal stewardship program. We don't surrender; we act. We get to write our own signatures on a check, or sign up for a committee, or put our name on a pledge card. We are shackled to the ideal of self-sufficiency. But Jeremiah reminds us that in the heart, where it truly matters, we don't write the signature, God does: "I will write it on their hearts; and I will be their God, and they shall be my people." If we clear some space for God, we may find that, buried beneath all the activity and ceaseless motion, there lies a heart that truly beats only in response to God's powerful rhythms. Only by surrendering our will to God's, only by yielding our activity to God's providence, only by keeping Sabbath time instead of restless time, only by resting in the presence of the One who made us are we replenished and nourished with love.

In the low pressure zone of Lent, a few weeks before the thundering storms of crucifixion, I invite you to pause. Before you pay the bills, first pay attention. Before you sign a check, look at God's signature inscribed upon your heart. Instead of rushing breathlessly to another meeting, let the breath of God blow some fresh air into your busy calendar. Before you worry about a budget, whether it's yours or the congregation's, bask for a moment in the lavish extravagance of God's grace.

In other words, let God take the initiative, and then follow as God rightly leads you. For the promise of the Lord is sure: "A new heart I will give you, and a new spirit I will put within you; and I will remove from your body the heart of stone and give you a heart of flesh" (Ezek. 36:26).

I recently met with John, a young man in our confirmation class. We were wrestling with a difficult question, namely, how do we experience God? I asked John to draw a picture of his earliest image of God. John drew a picture of a bearded old man, standing on a windswept mountain with outstretched arms. This was the traditional image of God, the God of Sinai, the God who carved the terms of the covenant on an external stone tablet. Then I asked John to draw a picture of how he currently experiences God, and this time John drew a picture of a road going toward the horizon, a line between a lot of activity. Standing on the side of the road were people, still and motionless. John drew himself in the picture as one of these people. Moving between the people and touching them all at once in their very center was a pulsating luminous ball, flashing with light. John pointed to the ball and said, "That's God."

For a few quiet minutes, I marveled at John's second picture. He had discovered, in his own way, that God was present not only in our activity, but also in our stillness, not only in our questing and acting, but also in our quiet surrendering. John's picture pointed to a God who touches the human heart, who comforts, guides, and gives life.

This, indeed, is the heart of the matter, and here in the "low pressure zone" of Lent, the best word I can name to encircle the many ways we respond to such infinite, abundant love is stewardship.

WHATEVER?
Philippians 4:1–9

James Moiso

Think on these things . . .
    I wonder when Oregon State University will win another football
    game—or the University of Oregon, for that matter.
Think on these things . . .
    When am I ever going to get organized enough
    to feel like I'm in control of my life?
Think on these things . . .
    I'm so proud of my kids and how they are growing up.
    I just hope I can keep them out of trouble.
Think on these things . . .
    I'm afraid to go anywhere at night.
    Do you know how dangerous it is?
Think on these things . . .
    AIDS. Oh, no, not AIDS.
Think on these things . . .
    Violence. Violence and so much easy sex.
    That's all I see on TV. I complain, but I still watch it.
Think on these things . . .
    When will my parents let up on me? They're always pressuring me to
    do something, be somebody. I don't know how much more I can
    stand.
Think on these things . . .
    Retirement's coming. I say I look forward to it.
    But what will I do with myself? I can't just sit around.
Think on these things . . .

Do you think I'm still attractive?

If I didn't color my hair, you'd see how old I really am.

Think on these things . . .

When are they going to stop giving me more work?

With downsizing, I'm already doing two jobs.

I'll never get it all done.

Think on these things . . .

I wonder if I have enough money. I don't ever want to burden my children. They have enough to worry about.

Think on these things . . .

I really feel out of touch if I don't watch the news.

But it's all so negative. What's our world coming to?

Think on these things . . .

Sex. I wonder if anyone will ever really love me.

Think on these things . . .

Now, is the soccer game at 10 or 11? When are the practices this week? How am I going to get to my exercise class if you have to be at school? What about dinner?

Think on these things . . .

Days seem so long, just sitting.

I used to do so much, but now, what with my health and eyesight, golden years are really rusty. Seems like all I do is go to the doctor.

Think on these things . . .

All I ever see are kids in trouble, abused, screwed up.

Dysfunctional families. People acting out pain in violent ways.

Think on these things . . .

It would have been easy for the church at Philippi to focus on all that was troubling. They were a tiny minority in a sea of unbelievers. They were persecuted, some ostracized from their families, some suffering economic consequences for claiming Christ. More than that, they were a divided community. No wonder Paul repeatedly urged a unity of spirit. In today's scripture passage, we hear about two leaders in disagreement, two women who were so at odds that the well-being of the congregation was threatened. All was not well in this fledgling family of faith. More than that, their esteemed founder and leader, the one they trusted, on whom they depended, was imprisoned in Rome. Where was God? If this was the gospel, if the risen Christ was all powerful, how could all this happen? Think on these things, all these things . . .

The apostle Paul knew that life first of all is a spiritual journey. Life is not a work party, or a joy ride, or a contest for the survival of the fittest. Above all else, God has so wonderfully made us that we are creatures who require nourishment, physically and spiritually. So, to his beloved and beleaguered congregation, Paul addressed the stewardship of their spirits, individually and together. "Guard your hearts and minds in Christ Jesus by continuing to think, judge, plan, resolve your life together in these things."

When we read these verses, the eighth verse particularly resonates within: "Finally, beloved, whatever is true, whatever is honorable, whatever is just, whatever is pure, whatever is pleasing, whatever is commendable, if there is any excellence and if there is anything worthy of praise, think about these things."

There are so many things that tempt us, things that can fill our hearts and minds, if we let them. There is music that denigrates people and extols destructive power, and there is music that celebrates life in its wondrous facets. We can focus on what's wrong about life and blame God, or we can consider what is right and give God glory. We can enjoy the exposés of human weakness and evil, or we can marvel at human achievement and generosity in spite of weakness.

By the way, when Paul calls us to think about the good things, he is not making an appeal to shallow positive thinking. He knows deep inside that we will nourish our spirits with something; that cannot be helped. He calls us to choose the food of compassionate living, to choose the drink that builds community, because this is God's highest intention in Christ Jesus.

Gregory of Nyssa, a fourth-century church leader, cared deeply about the stewardship of our spirits. "We are in some manner our own parents," he said, "giving birth to ourselves by our own free choice in accordance with whatever we wish to be . . . molding ourselves to the teaching of virtue or vice."[1]

The decision to set our minds on higher things is an act of will. It is a decision we make every day, consciously and unconsciously. It is a way of thinking and living. As we choose to guard our hearts and minds in Christ Jesus, the healing and redemption in Christ will break in upon us, and our lives will reflect it. "Whatever" we choose to think on makes all the difference.

A marvelous event took place recently, and I almost missed it. Thirty-three years ago, a young student, Vivian Malone Jones, defied Governor George Wallace and the threats of hundreds of other students and adults. Under protective guard, she and a single male student integrated the University of Alabama for the first time. The news image of a snarling George Wallace and two very vulnerable students is imprinted in my memory. This week, Vivian Malone Jones received the Wallace Foundation award, honoring her contributions to society. Thirty-three years after that tense confrontation, the family of George Wallace admitted its mistake. It took public action toward reconciliation and healing. Vivian Malone Jones expressed forgiveness and thanked God for this possibility. Two images are before us: we can choose to think on the angry, bigoted Wallace or on what is true, just, and praiseworthy in life, even in his.

One evening, as my mother lay dying in the hospital, she became agitated. We all wanted to do something to make her more comfortable, but because of medication, she was in and out of awareness. Then it came to me: Psalm 23. So I took her hand and asked her to say it with me, "The Lord is my shepherd . . ." It was as if I had touched something deep inside, something that had been thought on. Phrases came to her lips, memorized and repeated through the decades. She stopped here and there, haltingly repeating, "Shall not want . . . shall not want . . . he restores my soul . . . restores my soul . . . the house of the Lord forever . . . forever." And a peacefulness returned to her.

We are miraculous creatures of God, and it makes a profound difference "whatever" we put in our minds and hearts. Make every moment of every day count as you shape your spirit, and our spirit together, in Christ Jesus. Rejoice in everything that is good and wonderful, in the vast array of abundant gifts we have together. Worry less and dream more. Complain less and laugh more. As we rejoice in whatever is true, honorable, just, pure, and gracious, we will have the strength to face that which is tough and ugly in life. If we focus on the negative, we will have no strength to confront it or to overcome it. Our spirits will be too malnourished, fed with food that stunts and kills. Choose carefully whatever it is you think. We are stewards of our spirits, on a journey of faith together. So, this first day of the new week, I call on you to rejoice in the journey. There is so much that nourishes life. I invite you to rejoice especially in the understanding that God is God, active among us in Christ Jesus. Amen.

THE SPIRITUAL DISCIPLINE
OF GIVING

THE TOP FIVE REASONS WHY I DON'T TITHE YET
2 Chronicles 31:1–10

William G. Carter

On a shelf in my study, there is a three-volume work titled *Dictionary of New Testament Theology*. It is a helpful set of reference books, containing an expository article on every significant word in the New Testament. If you like to learn about words, this is the reference for you. You can read about the three different Greek terms for love, trace the historical development of the concept of grace, or gain a wider perspective on the dynamics of forgiveness. In preparation for my sermons, I frequently turn to those volumes for help.

It was a natural step, then, to see what the dictionary had to say about tithing. I have never before preached a sermon on tithing, so I opened volume 3 and began to flip through the pages. I found the entry, but not without noting the heading for the very next article. There they were: on one page, an article on "tithing," and on the very next page, an article on "torment." I thought, "Now, that will preach!"

Members of our congregation have not complained that I have never preached on tithing. Most people around here, myself included, would hear a sermon on tithing as a sermon on torment. We don't want anybody to tell us what to do with our money. It troubles us. Maybe that is why I have never before preached a sermon on tithing. Perhaps that is why I do not tithe. At least, not yet.

We cannot avoid the topic in the Bible. Tithing is a practice that appears throughout the pages of scripture. Most of the time, the Old Testament talks about tithing, often as a teaching or a rule. For instance, Moses lays down the Law in Leviticus 27:30: "All tithes from the land, whether the seed from the ground or the fruit from the tree, are the LORD's; they are holy [i.e., set apart] to the LORD."

Other times, the practice occurs in a story, like our passage for today from 2 Chronicles. This is a snapshot from Israel's family album. Israel was cleaning its own house, and the passage describes the preparation of the people to rededicate the Jerusalem temple by rededicating themselves to the One whom they worshiped: they celebrated the Passover and remembered how God brought them out of slavery.

Next they reaffirmed what they would *not* worship. They pulled down the sacred poles, which were shrines dedicated to the idols in their surrounding culture. God's people have a different story from those around them. They follow a different script. So the people cleared their heads and hearts.

Then they appointed servants to remind them that they worship God alone. The people of God do not belong to the idols who make empty promises that cannot be fulfilled. So they selected clergy to remind them of God's claim on their lives.

Finally they tithed their possessions. That is, they gave one-tenth of what they owned to support the temple, for the temple is the place where they heard, and responded to, the God they worshiped. We do not know if the temple had a budget, even though somebody in the institution must have managed its income and expenses. But we know they went to the temple to find life's deepest meaning. Affirming how they belonged to God, the people of Israel gave to the temple a share of everything they had: grain, wine, oil, honey . . . and money.

There is no shortage of Bible stories about tithing. Yet I do not tithe. At least, not yet. I need to do a little spiritual house cleaning of my own. That explains the title of this sermon: "The Top Five Reasons Why I Don't Tithe Yet." Once in a while a preacher like me needs to confess the unfinished pieces of his life. In that spirit, and with the hope that others will have a chance to work through their own excuses, let me list the top five reasons why I don't tithe yet.

Number five: I don't tithe yet because the church has not talked about tithing very much.

I realize I blame the church rather than myself. That can be a cop-out, but when was the last time any of us heard a sermon about tithing? When was the last time you heard a Presbyterian talk about making a tithe? Usually we talk about giving in general and never say anything specific. Or we talk about supporting a church budget, as if that were the only thing that mattered. That is not the case in other churches. Go to an Assembly of God church, for instance, and you will hear that tithing is the standard expectation of every church member.

The practice of tithing can become legalistic and lifeless, as we know.

Nevertheless the expectation is clear in other communions, and everybody knows it. Presbyterians don't talk about tithing very much. Perhaps the topic strikes a little too close to home. Statistics reveal the average Presbyterian makes more money than the average member of any other denomination (except Episcopalians). Yet, on the average we give only two or three percent of our income to the church. In our affluence, we have softened the historic demands of our faith.

Did you hear about the Presbyterian who tithed regularly when he first started his business? He made the commitment to give 10 percent off the top. Then his business really began to take off. Suddenly he was making a thousand dollars a week more than he used to make. His business expanded, and a greater share of his income went toward overhead costs. He didn't have the margin to tithe any more. It bothered him. He went to his pastor to tell his sad story. The pastor listened and said, "I have an idea: let's pray about it." The man eagerly agreed. The minister prayed, "Lord, please reduce this man's salary so he can tithe again."

Whether we talk about tithing or not, the scriptural demand is still present.

Number four: I do not tithe yet because I am stuck on the idea that giving ought to be useful.

Did you notice what the people gave in that story from 2 Chronicles? Grain, wine, oil, honey, and money. Also, the produce of the field, cattle, and sheep. When they gave these possessions, they piled them up in heaps! For four months, says the writer, they piled up everything. Just imagine the smell of the sheep alone! That doesn't seem useful; if anything, it sounds downright wasteful. What will a temple do with all that stuff? As Judas Iscariot said, "Couldn't we sell these things and give the money to the poor?" (John 12:5). At least that would be useful.

We do not always know what to do when somebody offers a gift and refuses to dictate its use. When that happens, it seems too much like . . . a gift.

A group of ministers from various denominations gathered recently to talk about stewardship. While they met, something unforgettable happened. A conference speaker was talking about generosity. To prove his point, he pulled a one-hundred-dollar bill out of his wallet and said, "Lord, I love you more than anything else. To prove it, I'm going to offer this money to you." He put the one-hundred-dollar bill in an ashtray and set it on fire. A number of underpaid ministers sat in stunned silence, their hands gripping their chairs as that little green piece of paper burned up. I am certain a few of them were thinking, "If he has a hundred bucks to waste as a burnt sacrifice, why doesn't he give it to me?" Then the glimmer of understanding began to dawn on the group: the speaker really was giving his money to God.

Some of those present found it disturbing because it was not useful, much in the same way that singing a hymn is not useful. We expend a lot of breath when we sing, and we do it because we love the One we sing about. And we are likewise called to give our money because we love the One to whom we offer it. True generosity cannot be reduced to a matter of being useful.

As I watched a one-hundred-dollar bill go up in flames, offered as a burnt sacrifice to a holy God, it struck me as a holy moment.

Number three: I do not tithe yet because I keep forgetting that my entire life is a gift from God.

I don't know if you have ever gotten forgetful like this, but it can happen. If I am honest, I admit that I think some things in my life come from God, and everything else is earned by my own efforts. The story from 2 Chronicles pushes us farther. It will not let us think merely about money. It pushes us to reflect on our entire lives. The people brought their crops and gave a tenth. They herded their farm animals, picked the best-looking ones, and offered the first 10 percent. They offered food, and not merely the bruised apples or the dented cans of creamed corn. They offered the first fruits, the best food the land could produce. They gave these things, not because they had cash value (which they did), but because they were an essential part of everyday life.

If you wish to give a tenth of your zucchini crop to the church, we may not know what to do with it, but we will honor it as a gift to God. God wants us to give something of ourselves. God wants tangible evidence to show that we belong to him. When we give the first piece of what we have, we affirm that everything comes from God. What we do with our money matters deeply with God, because it exposes our values, our commitments—in some sense, it exposes our very lives!

Remember the old Jack Benny gag? A robber came up to Jack Benny and said, "Your money or your life!" Mr. Benny stood there motionless.

Again the robber repeated, "Your money or your life!"

Mr. Benny replied, "I'm thinking! I'm thinking!"

We make distinctions that do not exist in the eyes of God. Our money or our lives? Given the choice, God wants our lives . . . and that includes our money, along with everything else.

Number two: I do not tithe yet because giving is not always a first priority or a regular discipline.

There is little I can say to defend myself. It reflects my own lack of discipline. The people of Israel gave their first fruits. They gave first to God. Every other commitment followed. By contrast, I pay other bills first and give God a little bit of the leftovers. Tithing begs the question: who comes first?

As God would have it, I received a phone call from a friend while I was working on this sermon. My friend asked what the sermon was about, and I told him. It was a big mistake. You see, he tithes. He thinks I should. He thinks all of you should, too. In the middle of his speech, he said something that made sense. He said, "There are a lot of creditors who want a piece of me and my paycheck. There are all sorts of other concerns that compete for my attention and my money. But I write out my check to the church first, before I pay anything else. It is my way of saying that I belong to God before anybody else can get a piece of me."

His comment struck me, because it moves tithing from being an obligation to a statement of faith, a declaration of allegiance, a response to the care and protection of the Lord of your life. When we give our money to the church, we participate in the Lord's work, whether we contribute to the overhead costs for the religious establishment, or extend what the Lord is doing in the world, or underwrite those things that our Lord values and honors.

Most of all it is a way of saying, "I belong to God before I belong to anybody else." And I believe that; at least, I think I do. Of course, I don't tithe. At least, not yet. Do you know why I feel that way? It has to do with the number one reason why I don't tithe yet.

Are you ready? Get a pencil and write this down. Here is the *number one* reason why I don't tithe yet: because I do not trust God enough. Or to put it another way: because I am afraid.

Fear is the issue, isn't it! If I tithe, will God catch me? Or will I face financial self-destruction? It is easy for me to add up all my financial commitments and put God last. My house costs $108,000. I pay $892 a month for the mortgage and taxes. The rusty Nissan is paid off, but the station wagon costs $262 a month. Utilities are another $250 a month, depending on how much time I spend on the phone. Then there are credit card bills (another $200 or so), groceries, diapers, gasoline, insurance. Where does God fit into my budget?

So what are we going to do? One response is to give to God a proportion of what we earn. Then we can make a commitment to grow in our giving until we attain a tithe.

For instance: if you work forty hours a week, calculate how much you make per hour. Then start by giving what you make for the first hour of your weekly work. That is one-fortieth, only 2.5 percent. It isn't a tithe, but we have to start somewhere. Once we make a commitment, we can grow into the fullness of generosity. What's to stop us? Only fear.

In a few minutes, I am going to try something: I will pull out my checkbook and write a check for one-tenth of what I earned this week. I have to start somewhere, and so do you. Maybe today is the day when you jump in and start tithing. If so, you would be saying, "God, you are the Lord of my life. I love you more than anything else, even more than my money. And to show my devotion, I give you the first ten percent of all that you've given me."

Here is a promise I will make with you today. This time next year, I will report to you how I am moving toward tithing. But here's the catch: I will be interested in knowing how you are coming along too. After all, we are in this ministry together, aren't we! If your answer is yes, I will have one less reason that I don't tithe . . . yet.

NOT AS AN EXACTION
2 Corinthians 9:1–7

Robert J. Elder

Judged by contemporary standards, the apostle Paul employed some strange fund-raising methods. In our text for today, Paul was busy encouraging the folks in Corinth to make an offering, to be diligent in stewardship, to do their best to give to the distressed saints in Jerusalem, but, curiously, he never said anything about the nature of their suffering. Isn't it strange that, in seeking an offering for suffering people, Paul mentioned so little about actual conditions of poverty in Jerusalem? What sorts of deprivation were they experiencing? Exactly how great was their need? He missed a chance to highlight something that could have increased the response of the people in Corinth, and I wonder why.

This is certainly not the way we go about raising money for charitable causes today. Paul needs some help here. If there is a disaster in the world, we see pictures on the news within hours. We depict suffering as vividly as possible. Everyone has been moved by the pictures on television of the distended bellies and ghastly living conditions of people in third-world countries. Television producers know, and so do we, that if people can see human suffering, they will become more compassionate and generous.

So if we were organizing Paul's appeal, we would encourage him to do things differently, to describe the suffering more vividly. How else would we change Paul's approach to make his stewardship campaign more effective? Perhaps we should urge Paul also to appeal to people's sense of obligation and duty.[1] All others are doing their share, he could say, and so should you. Paul could play on not only personal duty but institutional obligation too: "Your name is on the roll of this organization, and you should do your part."

But, when you think about it, this approach might not work. This sort of appeal portrays stewardship as dues paying, doing one's bit, being a loyal member of the local service club, and some may respond to this, but, to tell you the truth, not many. I can't get very enthusiastic myself about stewardship that presses obligation or duty, so I'd have a hard time trying to convince Paul to use this method.

If appeals to obligation aren't the way to go, maybe we could encourage Paul to appeal to self-satisfaction. Knowing we have done something good for someone else can give us a warm inner glow. Never mind that such gifts, while commendable, are really a thinly disguised way of giving to ourselves; this is a proven way to raise money. Many people, when motivated by self-satisfaction, by giving to themselves really, become extra generous and the gift to the church might be larger than we anticipated. But no, on second thought, this approach isn't all that good either—a warm inner glow only goes so far. So, I wouldn't advise Paul to go this way after all.

Maybe, then, I would tell Paul to appeal to people's sense of prestige. Paul could create a stewardship program for those who "care enough to send the very best." I once visited a church that had a large leather book on the chancel steps. I looked at the opened page, and it read, "Members who have pledged $2,000 or more to our church." The page wasn't blank, so this appeal to prestige seems to work. But, upon reflection, this is not the way to go either. Pride in giving can be good, of course, but it can also be dangerous. Prestige gifts advertise the glory of the giver, but most of us do not have the resources to be the most impressive giver anyway.

So maybe Paul had it right all along. Maybe Paul was wise to ignore fund-raising methods altogether. Instead of taking the low road, Paul persevered on the high road with a theological theme he raised at the beginning. The world might make its appeals for funds on the basis of need, obligation, self-satisfaction, prestige, sympathy—in short, on something people have done—but Paul focused his energy almost entirely on what God has done.

We can see Paul's emphasis on the work of God in the very first verse of our passage. Sometimes this verse is translated to say that Paul is writing to the Corinthians about the "offering for the saints." This makes it sound like Paul is interested in the offering plate, the Sunday collection. But Paul actually used the word *diakonia*, which means "service" or "ministry" (the root of our word "deacon"), and a better translation is: "I write to you about the service (or ministry) for the saints." Paul was not talking about mere fund-raising; he was talking about ministry in the name of God. Paul set the service to the poor within the context of service to God. It is a reality the church must always keep foremost in our prayers and actions, otherwise our congregation could degenerate into little more than another fund-raising organization.

I once asked a young girl busily engaged in selling some trinkets to raise money for an organization, "What is the purpose of your organization?"

She looked blankly at me for a moment. "Purpose?" Then, looking at the bag of goods she had grasped in her hand, she brightened up and said, "We make money and then spend it!"

The church could be in danger of becoming such an organization should the perennial temptations to find better fund-raising techniques ever overtake our calling to be faithful hearers and doers of God's Word. Fundraising has its place within our community. Money is needed to do good all over our world, and it must be raised or good will not be done. But our purpose is not to raise money and spend it. Our purpose is service, ministry in God's name. At the core of things, we are gathered together as a community of God's people to preach Christ and minister in his name. Paul called the offering a "ministry," for that is the only way in which he ever would have involved himself with it.

Later in the same passage, Paul said he hoped the gift the Corinthians had promised would come "not as an exaction but as a willing gift." Recently one of our Bible study groups was studying this passage, and they agreed that the word "exaction" was a good one. It sounds enough like the dentist's term "extraction" to make Paul's point even clearer. Paul wanted no part of an offering that was coerced out of people, an offering that required a good shot of novocaine so that people wouldn't holler quite as much as it was yanked out of them. His interest was in a willing gift, one given in response to the gifts of God and to the need of others.

So instead of trying to get Paul to adjust his methods of stewardship, perhaps we should pay attention to the ways Paul went about motivating the Corinthians to respond to God's gift of grace with their own ministering gifts:[2]

First, Paul's appeal was tactful. While saying "there is really no need for me to write," he wrote anyway, just as pastors often say, "You'll remember the story about . . . " and then tell it anyway since it is good to be reminded even of the things that are familiar. Response to God's grace is a constant need of God's people, and we need reminding.

His appeal was also positive. "I know that you are willing to help. I boast about you to the people of Macedonia." Paul was confident in the strength that God could give to the Corinthians, just as I am confident of the strength that God is ready to give us. Our church is engaged in countless acts of wonderful ministry, and I boast to my colleagues in the ministry about this church all the time. It is a foundation upon which we can build, and God is ready to give the energy supplied in our response.

Moreover, Paul's appeal was honest. What Paul said about the Macedonians and the Corinthians was true. Knowing of the strengths of the other, each could be stimulated to renewed strength of purpose. The Macedonians were prepared to give in spite of their poverty. The Corinthians expressed their willingness to take part in the offering before anyone else. These were strengths worth building on. This approach was so typical of Paul.[3] He would not lift up weakness in order to criticize one church to another; he lifted up strengths in order to praise one church to another. It's not a bad idea to try as we look around our own church for the many strengths that can serve as an inspiration to others as well as to ourselves.

Finally, Paul's appeal was direct. Paul spoke to the heart of the matter, to people's basic commitment to Jesus Christ. He wasn't just preaching; he was "meddling," speaking to the core of our values.

In many churches, stewardship programming follows this pattern:

> the committee is organized and meets regularly;
>
> assignments are made and carried out;
>
> budgets are developed;
>
> the ministry of the church is interpreted;
>
> sermons on stewardship are preached;
>
> challenges are extended.[4]

This looks like a complete stewardship program, but one crucial element is missing. In some fashion, we must be confronted with an inescapable decision about personal commitment. As someone notes, "To inform and nurture the people of God without confronting them with the cost of discipleship is to show ourselves as poor stewards."[5] This is no less the case in stewardship than it is in our decision to follow Jesus. At some point, someone has said to us, "Who is your Lord and Savior?"

Paul's appeal called for faithful gifts, heartfelt gifts, not guilt-driven gifts. God accepts our gifts not as an exaction—or an extraction!—on the basis of what we have to give, not on what we don't have. That is how it must be with our pledge commitment. The only really driving force comes from within, inasmuch as the love of Christ claims and directs us.

This day, and in the days to come, we are a called people, called to respond to the gracious love of Christ with hearts, minds, hands, and, yes, even checkbooks open to the leading of his Lordship. Let us give thanks and praise to God for his inexpressible gift.

HILARIOUS GIVING
2 Corinthians 9:6 – 15

Carlos E. Wilton

One day in 1888, a certain Norwegian businessman reached for his morning newspaper. Flipping through the pages, he received the shock of his life: he saw his own obituary.

It was all a terrible mistake, of course. The businessman's brother had died and a careless reporter, confusing the two of them, had composed an obituary for the wrong man. But because of that blunder, the businessman got a rare and disturbing glimpse of how he was viewed by the world, of what the world would say of him when he died.

He did not like what he read. To be sure, the facts of his life were described accurately enough, and all his impressive achievements were laid out in detail. Yet there was nothing there of his high principles—his beliefs, his values, the things he held most dear. Instead, the obituary focused on his inventions, his factories, his patents, and his great wealth. Decades before, he had created an explosive that he called "dynamite," and this weapon of destruction had made him wealthy and famous beyond his wildest dreams. The Norwegian businessman was the world-renowned Alfred Nobel.

But it was on the day he read his own obituary that Alfred Nobel began a new life.

He realized, reading about his own death, that the world saw his life as founded on violence and war, on blowing things to bits. Shocked, Nobel decided that this experience had given him a second chance, that it was an opportunity for resurrection and redemption. He began giving his money away. He made provision in his will for the Nobel prizes, rewarding those who had made the greatest contributions to humanity and peace. Today he is best remembered for humanitarian work, for the Nobel Peace Prize. Alfred Nobel, in effect, rewrote his own obituary.

Thank God for second chances! Praise the Lord that there are some occasions in life when we are given the sheer grace to see ourselves as we really are, to discern that something is wrong and to fix it.

Alfred Nobel was given a second chance, a second chance to use his money not for destruction but for joy, not for violence but for happiness. Stewardship gives all of us that same second chance.

"God loves a cheerful giver," writes the apostle Paul to the Corinthians. What a concept—that giving things away will make us happy! But it's God's honest truth. Anyone who's ever dug down deep enough to give a sacrificial gift, a gift that really costs something in money, time, or effort, and then has watched the smile of gratitude in the recipients, knows what it means to be a cheerful giver. It feels wonderful to give things away, if by giving we bring joy.

When Paul describes a "cheerful" giver, the Greek word he uses— *hilaron*— is related to our English word "hilarious." In some ways, I like "hilarious" better, for cheerfulness seems so low-key, so ordinary. "Cheerful" sounds like:

> "keeping the sunny side up"
>
> "looking on the bright side"
>
> "starting each day with a smile"

"Hilarious," on the other hand, is a great big belly laugh that swells and expands until the whole body is shaking. "Hilarious" is not a chuckle, but a guffaw; it's rolling in the aisles with merriment.

Is Paul really saying that we have a second chance with our money, a chance to give things away that can fill our lives with laughter? You bet he is! I've had it with this grim, tight-lipped attitude toward money in general, and stewardship campaigns in particular. Let's talk about the good news here!

Alfred Nobel had lots of money to give away, but it is not really the quantity that matters. Any of us can do it, even the poorest among us. The standard we hold up in the church is proportionate giving. That's giving based on a percentage of income, giving that's on its way to a tithe (or perhaps all the way there, or even beyond). Even if you're on one of those infamous "fixed" incomes, you can still give a "fixed" percentage of what God has given you. It's the act of opening the hand instead of closing it that's important; of seeing a need, large or small, and joyfully declaring, "I can take care of that."

There are two things I want to point out about hilarious giving: first, it operates from abundance, rather than scarcity, and second, it looks to the future, rather than dwelling in the present.

First, that vision of abundance. There's an East Indian fable about a rich man who is traveling far from home. A poor man notices his fine clothes and his bulging money bag, and decides to travel with him and look out for a way to steal his treasure.

Every night, in the humble inns along the roadside, the poor man unrolls his bedroll early and pretends to sleep. Then, as the rich man leaves the room to get washed up and ready for bed, the thief rummages through his belongings in search of the treasure sack. But he never can find it. As soon as he hears the rich man's footsteps, he leaps back into his bedroll, certain he's just moments away from finding the treasure. Every morning, the poor man once again pretends to sleep, until the rich man goes down for breakfast, yet morning is the same as evening: the thief never can find the money bag.

Day after day this goes on, until the two men finally reach their destination. As they are parting ways, the thief's curiosity gets the better of him. He admits to the rich man what he's been up to. "How have you eluded me for so long?" he asks. "Did you guess that I was out to rob you?"

"Yes," said the rich man, "I guessed that the very first night."

"Then where did you hide the treasure?"

"It was very simple," replied the rich man. "Every night, while you went to get cleaned up before bed, I slipped into the room and put my treasure in your pillow, and every morning after you had rifled through my belongings, I got it back."

Sometimes, in all our anxiety over finances, we too miss the treasure that is close at hand. If we are ever going to be hilarious givers, we've somehow got to stop chasing after treasure in every imaginable place, and realize that we have plenty of treasures close at hand.

I'm talking about a vision of abundance. I've mentioned this before, but it bears repeating, because I think it is especially hard to catch the vision of abundance.

"Do we," writes the theologian Parker Palmer, "inhabit a universe where the basic things that people need—from food and shelter to a sense of competence and of being loved—are ample in nature? Or is this a universe where such goods are in short supply, available only to those who have the power to beat everyone else to the store?"[1]

Scarcity or abundance? It's all in our choice of how we look at life.

Brother David Steindl-Rast, a writer in the field of spirituality, has another slant on this question. "Abundance," he writes, "is not measured by what flows in, but by what flows over. The smaller we make the vessel of our need . . . the sooner we get the overflow we need for delight."[2]

Many of us are trapped on the same treadmill of consumption that wearies our national American soul. As soon as "our cup runneth over," what do so many of us do? Why, we go out and buy a bigger cup! That means we are always living in an illusion of scarcity, always bemoaning the gap between what's in our cup and the rim— when in reality we, of all the peoples on this planet, are the most blessed financially (yes, even those of us on fixed incomes, even those of us trying to break into a career, even those of us with children in college, even those of us on food stamps).

If you or I believe we live in a world of scarcity, it is a sure thing we'll find giving to be a chore, a threat, even an insurmountable challenge. Yet if you and I catch the vision of abundance, hilarious giving will be our joy!

The second observation I'd like to make is that hilarious giving looks to the future. Alfred Nobel never saw a single one of his prizes awarded; the terms of his will stipulated that they would not begin until five years after his death. The Nobel Prizes were his gift to succeeding generations. Hilarious giving is always making possible a future for others.

There's an old Jewish fable about an elderly man who spent all his spare time planting fig trees. "You're a fool, old man," the villagers would tease. "Why are you planting fig trees? You're going to die before you'll ever bite into a single fig!"

"You are quite right," replied the old man. "Yet I have spent many happy hours sitting under fig trees and eating their fruit. Those trees were planted by others. Why shouldn't I make sure that others will know the same enjoyment I have had?"

Sounds pretty hilarious to me!

In downtown Seattle a few years back—though it could have been any city in this land—a man was walking down the street just a few days before Christmas. He came upon one of those Salvation Army kettles. As he approached the volunteer ringing the bell, he felt an unaccustomed spirit of generosity wash over him. Reaching into his pocket, he pulled out all his change. He dropped every last coin into the kettle with a smile.

The man turned to leave, but then he stopped. He reached into his back pocket, pulled out his wallet and emptied every last bill into the kettle as well.

Grinning like an idiot, he walked away with a bounce to his step. But about two blocks later, the bounce wore out. Suddenly it hit him! "What have I done?" he asked himself.

The man turned around, walked back to the old woman and asked for his money back. He got it, and left again, walking very quickly this time, head down, looking neither to the right nor the left.

"For two blocks," writes my friend Donel McClellan, "that man walked in the Kingdom of God. For two blocks he was free of the burden of his possessions. For two blocks he put other people above himself. For two blocks he was self-giving and generous. For two blocks he was blessed; but like most of us, he could not stand the uncertainty that goes with that much blessing. He wanted to continue to think that he is in control. He walked back, out of the realm of God and back into the well-worn grooves of his weary world."[3]

In the days to come, I hope you will consider what it means to walk in the kingdom of God. I invite you to consider what it would take for you to become a hilarious giver!

MONEY AND POSSESSIONS
AS ISSUES IN THE
LIFE OF FAITH

WHERE IS YOUR SADNESS?
Mark 10:17–27

Susan R. Andrews

Mark's story of the rich man who came to Jesus and asked about eternal life either fits us like a glove, or it has almost nothing to do with us at all. The story appears in what is sometimes called the "discipleship section" of the Gospel of Mark—those two or three chapters that seem specifically addressed to hard-core Christians, the ones who are serious about discipleship, the ones facing persecution, those who have given up father and mother and sisters and brothers and houses and children, the ones who have decided that this Jesus demands and embraces and empowers all of who they are.

Now, to tell the truth, there are two kinds of believers in this sanctuary today: the curious, hesitant kind and the already deeply committed kind. Some of us here today are still bystanders in faith, fascinated by this wandering preacher Jesus, but not yet committed to walk by his side. Others here have decided to take up the cross and are hungry for a full-bodied, deep-souled relationship with God.

God welcomes both kinds of believers to this place; God loves us all and nourishes us all in our journeys. However, for those who are bystanders, this story from Mark and this sermon today barely touch us at all. Another story, another day, but not this story, not today. But for those who wish to be committed and faithful disciples, for those who are traveling—even limping—along with Jesus on a journey toward the cross, then this story is crucial and it burns uncomfortably in our souls.

The story asks us to see ourselves in the light of this man who comes to Jesus. Mark tells us that this man was rich. Matthew tells us that he was a ruler. And Luke informs us that he was young. In other words, he had it all—money, power, youth—all the stuff, all the status, all the success that human achievement can bring. Yet his actions reveal that, like many of us, he did not, in fact, have it all. Eagerly he runs to Jesus and kneels before a scruffy itinerant preacher, a man he would probably not even invite to his table under normal circumstances, and he asks Jesus what he must do to have eternal life. Why such odd behavior? Maybe he was restless and empty, and wanted some spiritual nourishment. Or maybe, being the overachiever he was, he wanted a pat on the back and an A+ from God. Or maybe he still hadn't figured out the meaning of life and wanted some good answers. Who knows? But one thing is clear. Something is missing, and he asks for eternal life, not really knowing what he is asking. Jesus takes his question about eternal life seriously—as a question about the hunger for a full-bodied, deep-souled relationship with God—and the result was that the man got a surprise. The man did not know what he was asking for, and what he thought he wanted is not what he got, and what he got is not what he wanted.

The first surprise is that Jesus pointedly connected the question of eternal life to the issue of money. But in scripture that's not so unusual. In the Bible there are 2,350 verses dealing with money and possessions, compared to 500 verses describing prayer. One-sixth of what Jesus preached about dealt with money. If my sermon topics were chosen on these biblical proportions, you would hear eight or nine money sermons every year. So count your blessings! But for those of us here who are hungry for a full-bodied, deep-souled relationship with God, we cannot avoid the question of money, and this story about a rich man and his money is meant to stun us and to unsettle us and to make us pause uncomfortably before we fill out our pledge cards.

But it is not just a story about money; the second surprise of the story is that it is about a demanding kind of love. Mark tells us that Jesus loved the rich man. These are the most curious and powerful words in the text. After this proper, pious, perfect young man reels off his pedigree to Jesus, we are told that Jesus looks at him and loves him—a word in the New Testament that means to wish the best for him, to see and affirm the image of God in him.

We need to understand, though, how Jesus loves him. Not with a hug. Not with a special seat in heaven. Not with glowing references to insure a promotion to a more influential job. No, Jesus loves him by dousing his pride with cold, hard accountability. If the issue of money is unsettling in this story, it is equally unsettling to realize that Jesus' love is not always warm, fuzzy, comfortable, or comforting. As a mother, as a pastor, I know there are times when to love someone else with the love of Christ means to confront irresponsible and destructive behavior. It means to refuse to reinforce dependency or self-pity. It means to be tough and demanding. It means to encourage someone else to do for themselves what they want me to do for them instead. Yes, it means to allow a child to fail instead of doing the math problem for her. It means to say no to a couple wanting to get married, if my instinct tells me they will destroy each other. It means to allow a program to fall apart if someone has not followed through on their promised responsibility. It means to insist that two colleagues deal with each other directly instead of asking me to play mediator.

Not many of us do this tough love stuff very well because we tend to think that Christian love means giving people what they want when they want it, whether it contributes to their spiritual wholeness or not. But today Jesus shows a more demanding but better way. He loves the rich man by throwing the responsibility for salvation back into the man's lap. He tells him the one thing this particular believer needs to hear—the one thing he needs to do in order to open his life completely and wholly to God. Jesus loves him by pushing him toward maturity. And he loves him by giving him the freedom to say no. Yes, Jesus loves this rich young man even as the man walks away. He loves him by refusing to rescue him. He loves him by leaving him to wrestle with his own incompleteness. What this suggests is that we, too, may need to love others by refusing to rescue them. And God may love us by refusing to give us what we want. If today we too say no, if we too walk away from Christ's radical demands, if today we decide that this all-or-nothing business of the Christian faith is just too hard for us to stomach, our scripture assures us that God will still love us as we walk away. But that love may well leave us to wrestle and to stew in our own restlessness, in our own incompleteness, in our own sadness.

And that is the deepest surprise of this story, that, finally, what this story is most profoundly about is sadness. Yes, it is a story about money, and yes, it is a story about demanding love. But mostly it is a story about sadness—the inevitable sadness and sorrow and emptiness that eats away at all of us when we allow anything to separate us from God. The story tells us that the young man was shocked by Jesus' words and went away grieving, sorrowful, with deep sadness. He was being asked to move out of his carefully constructed world of security. He was being asked to strip his soul naked of all that he had achieved, and to trust not in things but in the mystery of God. He was being asked to redefine his whole sense of identity—from that of a self-sufficient, self-made man—to a God-dependent, God-made man. But he couldn't do it. He just couldn't do it. The familiarity and security of all that stuff and all that status was too dear to his heart. And so he walked away. But as he did so, a deep sadness washed through him, for he knew he was saying no to the only true source of joy and completeness that any of us can ever find.

All of us here at this church have been asked to fill out our pledge cards for the coming year. You have heard the needs of the church as we try to grow in spirit and compassion as a congregation. But the decision about how much money to give to the church has as much to do with your needs as it does with the needs of the institution. What do you need to do and to become in your life in order to move deeper into God's grace? How can this decision help you to begin to trust in something and someone beyond your own finite self? Our gospel story this morning poignantly reminds us that the American dream of stuff, status, and success is not where happiness and completeness are found. Accumulating, collecting, hanging on only distances us from the deep and wide Spirit of God. It is only through giving up, letting go, cleaning out that we make room for God to do something in our lives. And the more we are able to submit to the loving demands of God, the more we will be able to experience joy instead of sadness in our living.

A husband and wife, who were traveling around the world, saw in Korea one day a boy pulling a crude plow in a field, while an old man held the plow handles and directed it through the rice paddy. The husband was amused by the sight and took a snapshot of the scene.

"That's very curious," he remarked to the missionary who was their interpreter and guide. "I suppose they are poor."

"Yes," said the missionary. "That is the family of Chi Noui. When the church was built they were eager to give something to it, but they had no money, so they sold the only ox they had and gave the money to the church. This spring they are pulling the plow themselves."

The husband and wife were silent. Then the wife said, "That was a real sacrifice."

"They did not call it that," said the missionary. "They thought it was fortunate they had an ox to sell."

The two tourists had not much to say, but when they reached home, they took the photograph to the church and told their pastor about the incident. "We want to double our pledge to the church," they said, "and give us some plow work to do. We never knew what gratitude or joy or sacrifice really meant until now."

This day we are called to look deeply into our souls and discern what separates us from God. We are called to acknowledge the deep sadness that comes in our distancing ourselves from God. And then, knowing that God will not do for us what we must do for ourselves, let us ask for courage and grace to joyfully and sacrificially give all of who we are to the one who has given us life.

May it be so for you and for me—all to the glory of God.

MARVELOUS MAMMON
Matthew 6:19–21, 24

William G. Carter

A preacher recently began his sermon in a way that I want to begin my sermon today. After he read the scripture lesson, he looked out at the congregation and said, "The Bible is the church's book. It was written and preserved by the people of God. Through the Spirit, the Bible speaks a living Word to the people of God." Then he stepped out of the pulpit, his Bible in hand. He walked into the middle of the congregation, put the open Bible on a chair in the center aisle, and left it there.

Returning to the pulpit, the preacher pointed and said, "There it is. That's our book. Brothers and sisters, my job today is to raise a question: what are we going to do with the passage we just heard?"

That's how I want to approach the text this morning. It is a passage that comes right out of our book. Jesus said to his disciples, "No one can serve two masters. You cannot serve God and wealth." Sisters and brothers, what are we going to do with that passage?

It is one of the Lord's teachings about money, possessions, and wealth. The scholars who spend their lives counting up scripture verses tell us that Jesus spoke more about money, possessions, and wealth than he did about prayer. For instance:

> It is easier for a camel to go through the eye of a needle than for someone who is rich to enter the kingdom of God. (Matt. 19:24)

> Once upon a time, a nobleman went on a journey. Before he left, he entrusted three servants with different sums of money. (Matt. 25:14–15)

> Whenever you give money to the poor, do not sound a trumpet before you, as the hypocrites do. (Matt. 6:2)

The kingdom of heaven is like a king who settled accounts with his servants. He called in a man who owed him a whole lot of money. (Matt. 18:23–24)

Cure the sick, raise the dead, cleanse the lepers, cast out demons. You received without payment; give without payment. Take no gold, or silver, or copper in your belts. (Matt. 10:8–9)

According to the New Testament, Jesus talked repeatedly about money. He did not talk about it because he was a greedy preacher or a church fund-raiser. Rather, he addressed the issue because he knew how money can compete for our primary allegiance to God. In the words we heard a few minutes ago, "No one can serve two masters; you cannot serve God and wealth." Pick one or the other. We cannot choose both.

On a Sunday morning in worship, surrounded by familiar hymns and stirring prayers, that is an easy choice to make. I pick God; how about you? With the stained-glass shadow reflecting off my brow, I can easily choose God. There is no problem pointing a judgmental finger at the person who worships wealth.

When Roger B. Smith left as the chairman of General Motors in 1990, there was a vote at a stockholders meeting to almost double his pension to $1.2 million a year. The Michigan state treasurer shook his head with disgust. He said, "Roger, can't you eke out a retirement at $749,000 a year?"

Someone else said, "Mr. Smith, you will make $20,000 a week. In three weeks, you will receive more in retirement than what an average assembly line worker earns in a year." Nevertheless the vote was approved. Afterward Smith defended the pension by saying, "Sixty-one percent of corporations in this country have better pensions than General Motors."[1]

It is easy to point a finger at people like that. In our world, money means power, pleasure, security, and status. The world has its own version of the Golden Rule, namely, "Those who have the gold make all the rules."

Yet think of what money does to us. It stirs up fear, guilt, insecurity, greed, and selfishness. Wealth and possessions can enslave us with their dark power. They can demand our energy and devotion. They can lead us in destructive directions. As a wise teacher in the early church instructed, "The love of money is a root of all kinds of evil" (1 Tim. 6:10).

Some people love money more than they love God. As a Christian preacher, I want to point my finger at people like them. Then I realize three or four of those fingers are pointing back at me. That is unsettling.

I remember the day when my older daughter made the shift in morning television habits. She switched from the local public television station to the Nickelodeon network. It meant a shift from *Sesame Street* to *Rug Rats;*

or more to the point, from commercial-free public television to early morning commercials. She had become old enough to turn on the TV and to punch the channel buttons for herself.

That fateful morning I walked downstairs to find her staring at the television. "Good morning, Katie," I called. No answer. Her eyes were glued to a commercial for Barbie dolls. I don't think she had ever seen the commercial before. When she did speak, her little voice peeped up to nobody in particular, "I want that."

There was a Bo Peep Barbie. Katie said, "I want that."

How about a Foam and Color Barbie? "I want that."

A vision flashed of Barnyard Barbie with Nibbles the Horse. She responded, "I want that."

I stood there shocked. "Katie," I said, "you already have a dozen Barbies in your toy chest."

She broke the trance, turned with a smile, and said, "But Daddy, I want more." I pointed at her, and three or four fingers pointed back at me. We all want more. She learned that message from me. She picked it up from my culture.

What are we going to do with this text? "You cannot serve God and wealth."

Jesus means this, of course, in the largest possible sense. The word Jesus used for wealth is the Aramaic word *mammon*. "You can't serve God and mammon," he says. Mammon means "accumulated resources." Mammon means "piles of wealth." It is an inclusive word that includes money and possessions. If you have a copy of Carter's Concise Contemporary Dictionary, you'll find a good definition in that unpublished resource. The word *mammon* means "stuff," as in, "We have a lot of stuff around here." Or "Please go into your room and pick up all your stuff." Or closer to the point, "You cannot serve God and stuff."

These days, nobody I know would say, "Would you take the picnic cooler to the garage with the other piles of mammon?" They would say, "Please put this cooler in the garage with our other stuff."

It does not take much to realize what Jesus means when he refers to our stuff. We earn some money and buy things that hang around the home. We make a few investments here and there. We stockpile belongings in our closets. Having a house full of mammon does not make you a bad person. But it probably puts you under an enormous burden.

In our text, Jesus doesn't pronounce us evil if we have a toy chest full of Barbie dolls or a garage full of stuff. He does not speak against our possessions, per se. But he does speak against the way we stand taller when someone admires our fancy new wristwatch, or the way we scan the pages of a catalog when we already have a closet full of clothes, or the way we improve the house to keep up with the neighbors, or the hundreds of ways we infuse our stuff with meaning, significance, energy, and hope.

Who can point any fingers? Not me! I struggle with the power of my possessions, as you do. Why do I feel better when I buy a couple of new compact disks? Why do I get so depressed when the VISA bill arrives? My addiction to possessions, my hunger for money, my attachment to things must be fed over and over, and it wears me out.

It can be difficult to live in a town like ours, precisely because everything is so nice, so inviting, and so appealing. We regularly hear about the high school kid who got a new sports car as a graduation gift. We take for granted the beautiful houses and the manicured lawns and the electronically controlled dog collars. We delight in the quick trips to Disney World, the busy social calendars, and the upscale grocery stores. We enjoy these things so much that we do not even notice what a burden they can become. Did you know the darkest shadows in this town are cast not by poverty but by affluence? Mammon, which gives us so much enjoyment, can make us absolutely miserable. We expend so much energy working, earning, accumulating, keeping, and protecting our stuff. It is hard work. Mammon promises so much security. The only problem is we need a security system to keep our stuff secure. In the process, we are isolated from one another and cut off from the things that truly matter.

It comes as a jolt, therefore, for Jesus to speak so clearly: "You cannot serve God and mammon." You have to pick one or the other. This word he speaks is the sword he came to swing. This word is evidence of his radical pastoral care. His word can cut us loose. His word can set us free. Yet it comes with violent force. Take an inventory of all your worldly belongings some time, and it will not take a rocket scientist to realize what a burden it is to maintain them. They are never totally safe. As someone reminds us,

> Cash can be stolen; Porsches and Cadillacs rust; corporations collapse; moths eat dinner jackets. The "lifestyles of the rich and famous" are lifestyles of the always vulnerable and ever fearful. Moreover, there is always someone around who has more than we do, and the quest to keep up is an endless burden. Deadbolts, safety-deposit boxes, tax shelters— none of them finally protect what we really desire; none of them makes secure a treasure worthy of our hearts.[2]

This pronouncement of Jesus is calling us to think about our priorities. He invites us to examine where we put our energy. We must choose whom or what we're going to serve. Do we belong to God? Or do we belong to our stuff? Whose yoke are you going to allow to be put around your neck?

Mammon says, "Keep busy, work harder, earn your own way." God says, "Come, all who are heavy-laden and I will give you rest."

Mammon says, "Worry about your wealth, hover over the investment portfolio, act prudently." God says, "Loosen your grip, let go of it all, and get in step behind Jesus."

Mammon says, "Stash some money away for a rainy day." God says, "Who do you think sends the rain?"

Whom are you going to serve? It has to be one or the other. It cannot be both.

Mammon says, "Keep what you can to maintain your life. Grip it tight and don't let go." God says, "I will keep you."

Mammon says, "Do not rest for a minute. Keep looking over your shoulder." God says, "I brought you out of slavery. I have set you free."

Mammon says, "There is no such thing as a free lunch. You have to pay as you go." God says, "Why do you spend your money for that which is not bread, and your labor for that which does not satisfy? Come, eat and drink! Be satisfied by a table you did not set. Be nourished by the body and blood who gave himself up for you."

Whom are you going to serve? It has to be one or the other. "You cannot serve God and mammon."

This is the word of the Lord. It is sitting out there, right in the middle of our congregation. Every one of us has to decide what we are going to do. It is not an easy decision. It may not even be something we can decide today, once and for all.

Nevertheless the choice is clear. We can serve our stuff and become enslaved to it. Or we can loosen our grips, lighten our loads, and serve a living God who alone can set us free.

FREEDOM IN MINISTRY:
THE MONEY
Philippians 4:10–20

Fred B. Craddock

As many of you know, many scholars believe that this little piece of material originally was a separate note of thanks,
 sent to the church at Philippi,
 when Epaphroditus arrived where Paul was in prison,
 bringing a gift from the church.
There is much to be said for that position.
 The letter of Philippians does seem to be a collection
 of fragments of interchanges between Paul and that church,
 put together so that now it seems to be one letter.
 And yet, an argument can be made for it as one whole letter.

Whether you take this little piece in chapter 4—
 which has its own beginning and ending,
 and is thoroughly complete within itself,
 and seems chronologically to have been sent first
 before anything else—

Whether you take it to have been a separate letter,
or to be in the proper context where it is, doesn't matter.
 It is a note of thanks.

Just as certainly as it is a note of thanks,
it is a strange note of thanks.

In the first place, it's too long.
 Notes of thanks just aren't this long.
You can tell when you open the envelope it's a thank-you note,

because it opens top to bottom instead of side to side.
"Steve and I thank you for the fondue pot.
Of all the gifts we received at our wedding,
it is my favorite,
because that happens to be the only thing I can fix.
But I do plan to cook other things. Love, Carolyn."

Now that's enough.
And it doesn't matter that she says in all the notes,
"Your gift was the favorite one."
We want to feel good. This is the thank-you note.
The thing cost fourteen dollars!

Look at Paul's note: it's so long. It's a page and a half.
And it starts out the wrong way.
"I rejoice in the Lord that now, finally,
you have renewed your concern for me."
Now that's not the way to start.
The killer in there is the word "finally."
"You finally thought of me again."
That's not the beginning of a good thank-you note.

Paul realizes, once he puts it down that way,
"Oops—that's kind of barbed." So he softens it.
And then in the next sentence says,
"Well, you did have concern for me.
But you had no opportunity."
It's a beautiful image from the spring of the year.
"You were not bearing fruit because it was not the season."

And then he says, "Not that I complain of want . . ."
(Now this is the thank-you note!)
"Not that I complain of want.
I don't sit here in my cell,
rattling a tin cup across the bars,
saying, 'Has the mail come today?'
No, no, no, no.
I know how to get mail, I know how to get no mail.
I know how to receive packages.
I know how to sit here with no package.
I know how to have a lot. I know how to have nothing.
I know how to have plenty.
I know how to be totally without.
Because I have learned in whatever condition to be content.

    I am adequate in every situation
    through Christ who gives me strength."

"Not that I seek the gift . . ."
    (He can't quit, can he!?!)
"Not that I seek the gift.
I seek the credit that goes to your account because of the gift,
    because you really didn't give it to me.
    You gave it to God, a gift,
    an offering accessible and acceptable to God.
    And my God will supply every need of yours in Christ Jesus."

That's the thank-you note.
How would you feel if you received that?

"You Philippians know you were the only church
that entered into giving and receiving with me."
    This is an extraordinary relationship.
    For you know from the letters of Paul
    that he did not let churches give to him easily,
    slipping a few bills in his pocket as he came and went.
        No.
    He would spend his energy and risk his life
    raising money for the poor saints, famine-stricken.

But to give something to Paul?
    "I work with my own hands. I pay my way.
    You know, night and day I took care of myself.
    I needed the freedom to preach free of charge."

But the church at Philippi was honored above all other churches
in this one regard: he allowed them to give him a gift.
    "Even when I went to Thessalonica you alone helped me.
    Time and again, you helped me then.
    Not that I seek the gift. Not that I am in want.
    Not that I really needed it. It was good for you to give it."
That's the way he talked. How are we to understand it?
    This strange note of thanks in the latter part of Philippians
    has puzzled and fascinated students of this letter
    for centuries and centuries.
        It is unusual.

Part of its unusual nature can be attributed to the fact
that he's talking about money.

And Paul knows, as you know,
that you cannot discuss that subject in simple sentences,
just cause and effect, flattened out.
It is a complex matter.
    The Bible argues with itself.

Some of the writers in the Bible say
prosperity is a sign of God's favor.
    "The person who delights in the law of the Lord
    is like a tree planted by the water,
    and everything he does will prosper."
    "Show me a prosperous man, I'll show you a righteous man,
    because I have never seen a righteous man hungry,
    nor his children begging for bread."

As one of the great benefactors in the history of America
once said, "Show me a poor man, and I will show you a sinner."
But other parts of the Bible said, "No, the opposite is true."
    "Blessed are the poor. Blessed are the poor."
What did Mary sing?
    "He has filled the hungry with good things.
    He has sent the rich empty away."
Luke says, "A rich man and a poor man died.
    The rich man went to hell, the poor man went to heaven."
    You don't know anything else about them,
    except one ate and one didn't eat. And that was it.

The Bible argues with itself.
It's a very complex issue, just as it is with us.
    You can say "Thirty pieces of silver," and
    the ugliest scene of which we know anything comes to mind.
    Dark and gruesome, an ugly and foul story:
        "Thirty pieces of silver."
    What's the worst thing you could say about this man?
        "He did it for the money."
    What's the worst thing you can say about her?
        "Do you know what? She married him for the money."

And yet, there's hardly anything in the church that we do
that's more beautiful than giving our money as an offering to God.
    The tortured nature of the gift of thanks is due, in part,
    to the complexity of the subject.

Part of it is a kind of awkwardness of the apostle.

He stands before this gift from the church,
    and he's standing on one foot,
    and he's standing on the other foot.
And you can tell he's awkward.
"I thank you for the gift. You remembered me again.
I knew you thought of me. You just didn't have a chance.
    I didn't really have any wants.
    I don't really want for anything.
    I don't seek the gift, but I thank you.
You're the only church . . ."
    You see? You feel the awkwardness?

No wonder it's awkward.
Paul is at that moment, that rare juncture in human life,
    that is the most fragile, and yet the strongest,
    the most beautiful with the possibility of being the ugliest
    of any transaction we can ever know:
        the giving and the receiving of a gift.
That's a tender moment. It is a beautiful moment.

The New Testament thinks of that as such a beautiful moment that,
    at times, it will use exactly the same word
    for giving it and for receiving it. The word is *charis*.
    We translate it usually "grace."
        It can be translated "gift."
        It can be translated "thanks."
    You don't know whether it's being given (thanks),
        being received (grace), or being given (gift).
            Eucharist—that's it!
            Charisma—that's it!
            Charismatic—that's it!

The whole thing is one word,
    that marvelous transaction, which in its most beautiful form
    is an exchange in which the same quality and temperament
    characterize the person who receives and the person who gives,
    and no difference, really, is made.

No wonder the apostle is awkward here.
    He is at the juncture of the most beautiful
    and the most rare moment we know.

But there is another factor here.
Paul says, "I have learned to be content."

And he uses a Stoic word.
"With reference to things in this world,
    I learned to be apathetic. To have no feeling.
    To make the heart a desert and call it peace."
"I don't have any feelings in this matter."

There are people who arrive at that.
    Some after very painful experiences,
    of totally losing all appetite for anything.
        Not that it's a virtue,
        but they just lose all appetite for anything.

I've wondered if, perhaps, that might have been
the case of the rich ruler the Gospels tell about,
falling at the feet of Jesus: "Good Teacher, what must I do?"
    I wonder if he had reached that point.
Maybe going home from work in the afternoon
    with his beautiful robes,
    children on the street grabbing at his sleeve,
        "Penny, mister, mister, penny? We're hungry, mister.
        You give us . . . ?"
    "Get away, kids, you'll get my clothes dirty."
    And he gets home just in time to hear his wife say,
        as she scrapes plates of food into the disposal,
        "I don't know what I'm going to do to get
        those kids of ours to eat."
And he's just sick of it.
    The magnificence of life's promise,
    lost in the poverty of its achievement.
        "And the very thing I thought I wanted I have,
        and I don't want it at all."

Like Macbeth wading through blood, even of relatives,
to get the throne of Scotland.
    And when he gets it, what do you see?
    An old man sitting on the side of his cot,
        twirling a crown in his fingers.
    "How stale, flat, and tasteless
    are all the uses of this present world.
    It's an unweeded garden—Fie on it!"

The awkwardness in this thank-you note—what is it?
If I didn't know better, I'd say,
    "Here's somebody who's had a bad experience with gifts,
    and doesn't want to get too involved."

"Thanks for the gift, but, but I really didn't need the gift."
You have that feeling.
  Some of you know what that's like, because
  some of the ugliest things that ever happen involve gifts.
  Gifts can be very painful, treacherous, and demonic.
Gifts can!

When I was briefly in the parish,
a painful thing occurred in the membership.
  He was an officer in the church, and did well at it,
  but he was gone most of the time. His work took him away.
  His wife spent most of her time ironing, washing and ironing,
    washing and ironing, white shirts for him.
    Packing the suitcase. Emptying the dirty clothes.
    Washing them, putting them back in the suitcase.
  He was on the road most of the time.
  She began to discover in the clothing
  the evidence that he was having an affair.
    She was convinced of it.
  One day when she could explode, while he was home for lunch,
  she dumped the whole thing on him.
    She told me later he just sat there and stirred his food.
    Didn't eat anything. Didn't say anything. And left.
  He came in at three o'clock in the afternoon, called her name.
    She said, "I'm in here." She was doing some needlework.
  He walked in and said, "This is for you,"
  and tossed something into her lap.
    She picked up two keys.
  He said, "Look out there!"
  And outside she saw a new yellow Plymouth convertible.

She stopped to see me on the way to the lawyer. And she said,
  "I think I would have been able to forgive his infidelity.
  But I could not forgive him the gift.
  What did he think I was?"
    Gifts can be very painful.

When I was in third grade, the government had a hot-lunch program
if you could prove that you deserved one.
  It was a free-lunch program, so I got my credentials together,
  and established myself before the government,
    and they said, "You get a hot lunch."
And this is the way it worked.

Our teacher (bless her heart, she intended nothing wrong by it)
said, "Now boys and girls, the bell rings at five till twelve.
    Those of you getting free lunches, stand beside your desks.
    March to the cafeteria.
  The second bell will be at ten after twelve.
    Those of you buying your lunches, stand beside your desks.
    March to the cafeteria."
Five till twelve, the bell rings and I sit there.
  Because there's something worse than being hungry,
  and that's walking in front of your friends as a freeloader.
    If you're ever going to do something nice for somebody,
    please lay it gently on their pride . . .
    because that may be all they have.

You almost get the impression that Paul has been burned by gifts.
I don't think he has, but he surely is ginger in his comments.
  What is it?
I don't think he's tiptoeing at all. In my judgment,
  his expressions about the money,
  or whatever the gift was that they sent to him,
  are the expressions of a man who is *free*.
  He is absolutely free in relation to things. To money.

His freedom is not the freedom of a spiritualist,
  who translates everything into spiritual terms,
  and then laying "his finger beside his nose,
  up the chimney he rose."
    Like a gnostic of some sort.
  I don't know when we're going to get it straight in the church
  that it is not enough to rail against physical indulgence.
    There is also spiritual indulgence.
  And to wallow in spiritualism is just as debilitating—
  perhaps more so—than in physical things.
    He doesn't do that.

He doesn't handle the problem of money as a crusader.
  The difficulty with being a crusader
  (and Paul, I don't think could ever have been a crusader)
    is that a crusader lets the opposition
    or the problem or the issue determine the agenda.
  And Paul brought his agenda with him,
    his relationship to God in Jesus Christ.
  You see, the crusader always asks only one question,

as the crusader goes out into the world,
ferreting out the problem: "Who is it? Who is it? Who is it?"
But the Christian asks a question the crusader never asks.
The Christian doesn't always ask, "Who is it?"
The Christian asks, "Is it I?"

Paul isn't solving his problem as a moralist,
though he was interested in moral issues.
He doesn't solve it as a moralist,
who reduces the world to a set of bad habits,
and then enjoys not doing them.

Paul handles it another way. He expresses his freedom.
He is free from having to have money.
He is free from the illusion of all that it will do for him.
He's learned that's not true. He doesn't have to be wealthy.
How did he learn?
He says, "I've been initiated into the secret."
I don't really know how he learned it.
He says, "I know how to have a lot, how to have nothing.
I don't have to have a great deal."

Some of the really pitiful things you run into in the world
are scenes where people have not learned that yet,
where people haven't gotten the secret yet.

You see them in stores:
"I'd like to buy some time."
"We don't have any time,
but we can sell you a clock."
"Can I buy a friend here?"
"No, no, don't have any friends.
We can sell you a companion for the night."
"I'd like to buy a drop of rain."
"No, can't sell you any rain,
but we can have some water piped to your house."
"Can I buy some salvation here?"
"Oh, no. Got some nice Bibles. Sell you a Bible?"

See a man in a hospital corridor
with a fistful of twenty-dollar bills,
going up and down,
stopping every orderly and every nurse:
"My wife's in 306, in there under the oxygen tent.
I can't lose her now. We've been married thirty-three years.

There's a little something extra
if you'll check in on her once in a while.
Run in . . ."
    "Look, we'll take care of your wife. Put your money away."
"Well, just . . ."
He doesn't understand, does he?
He doesn't understand that the fundamental fabric
of human relationships is totally unrelated to money.
How sad it is to think that giving will do it,
or not giving will destroy it!
    The mother who puts a ribbon in her little girl's hair
doesn't put it in there to make her pretty.
She puts it in there because she is pretty.
And when you give a gift to somebody, it's not "in order to."
It's "because of."

Paul has learned that. And you know, he has learned to be absolutely free
from the need to be poor.
    "I know how to have a lot. I know how to have nothing.
I can take it either way."
He doesn't have to be either way. He doesn't have to be wealthy,
but remember, he doesn't have to be poor.

I used to think just being poor was a virtue.
    We used to have evangelists come to our town.
And I liked to hear them preach those sermons against wealth.
They knew everybody in the house was as poor as Job's turkey and mad
    about it.
And they have these sermons against the rich.
The assumption was, if you have money, bad news for you!
And if you don't have money,
you're going straight in through the pearly gates.

They preached those marvelous sermons, and in those apostrophes,
    those flights of oratory against the wealthy:
"Oh, with your big house on the hill,
    racks of shoes in every closet,
    room and bath for everybody, enough for all the neighbors!
But the day will come
    when all of that will turn to a box of rags,
And the roof will leak and the rent is due.
    Then where will you be?"

And then he paints this scene of one little room up over a store,

one string of light cord with a fifteen-watt bulb,
and lying across a mattress without a sheet,
and on the floor, old cigarette butts floating in stale beer.
And we said, "Sic him, preacher! Yeah!"
Lord, help the rich! They got theirs now, we get ours later.

You know, the trouble with that mindset
is that a person who has no money can be as materialistic
as someone who has money.
There are two kinds of people who worry about money:
those who have it, those who don't have it.
And there's many a child reared at a wealthy table,
and many a child reared at a poor table,
and they hear the same conversation,
nothing but money, money, money.
"Because we have it," or "if we had it."
Money, money, money.
You can inflate in the opinion of those children
what money will do and it will not do.

"I don't have to have a lot," Paul says.
"I don't have to be poor,
and I don't have to be rich.
Because I have learned the secret that has absolutely set me free
from the destructive power of this grasping, grasping thing."

He learned in that mystery
what Flaubert was later to say in that marvelous line,
"Of all the winds that blow on love,
the demand for money is the coldest and most destructive."
"I can have it; I can not have it,
because I have learned something else."

Paul uses an unusual expression in talking about that relationship with
Christ.
"I have been initiated into the secret (or 'the mystery')."
Do you have any idea what that is? The secret?
"I've been initiated into the mystery."

It happened in our family
that our daughter graduated from college
in the same year our son graduated from high school.
In a smooth move, I decided on gifts for both at the same time.
It would be the same gift.

I wanted to give them a poem.
  But I didn't want to hand them this poem,
  you know, photocopied or something.
So I went to the university, and in the art department,
  there was a calligrapher who wrote it on that brown paper
  that makes everything look like it's real old.

It was a Yiddish poem called *"Der Icher"*;
in English, "The Main Thing."
  I wanted to give them a beautiful copy of this poem.
She made this in a beautiful scroll for me, ten dollars apiece.
  And I went by the dime store and got the frames.
  It cost me about twelve or thirteen dollars a kid.
    But when it's your own kids, you blow it all, you know.
  Wrapped those up, put them on the bed.
  After their ceremonies,
  and we took all the pictures we wanted to take,
  they opened gifts,
  and they saved Daddy's gift to last, because it looks small,
  but they know there's really something in there . . .

So they get to my packages and they open these poems.
I can see the disappointment. I said, "Go ahead and read it."
  I said, "John, read the poem."
    He read the poem.
  I said, "You get it?"
    He said, "I don't get it."
  I said, "Laura, you finished college.
  Explain the poem to your young brother."
    And she read it and she said, "I don't get it."
  I said, "Well, just think about it. It will come to you."
  And so, they took those gifts.

Last time I was in Laura's house in Oklahoma,
  it was on the wall in the den. I said, "Do you read that?"
  And she said, "Every once in a while I read it."
  I said, "Do you get it?"
  She said, "I don't get it."
And I recently saw it hanging in the kitchen at John's.
I said, "John, do you read that?"
  And he said, "Yeah. What does that mean?"
Ah, they'll get it. It's the secret. It's the secret.

The poem says,

If your outlook on things has changed,
    this is not the main thing.
If you feel like laughing at old dreams,
    this is not the main thing.
If you recall errors of which you are now ashamed,
    this is not the main thing.
Even if you know what you're doing now
you'll regret some other time,
    this is not the main thing.
But beware, light-heartedly, to conclude from this
that there is no such thing as the main thing.
    This is the main thing.

And they said, "What is the main thing?"
    I've never told them. I'm going to tell you.
    I hope you won't tell them. I want them to figure it out.

But as far as I'm concerned, in all seriousness,
to be initiated into the secret of the fundamental relationship
with God that sets you free is gratitude.
I have never known a person grateful,
    who was at the same time small,
    or mean, or bitter, or greedy, or selfish,
    or took any pleasure in anybody else's pain.
        Never.

I was thinking that if I were on a search committee,
    looking for a minister for the church,
    and we were talking about, and with, a certain person.
I really think before I would even ask
    (and you know how important this is to me!),
    before I would even ask, "Can this person preach?"
        I think I would ask,
        "Is there any evidence that this person is grateful?"

"I have been initiated into the secret.
I thank God that you have revived your concern for me.
I'm not in want.
I'm content, because in every situation in life,
I'm adequate because of Jesus Christ."
You can call it "grace."
You can call it "gift."
You can call it "gratitude."
But that, my friends, is the heart of the matter.

CHOOSE, THIS DAY, WHOM YOU WILL SERVE
Joshua 24:1–3a, 14–25

Roger P. Howard

Choices, choices, choices. "Whatever you choose" is the slogan of our age. Every day we have placed before us many choices, almost too many. Television cable channels keep expanding—there are now hundreds of options. On the Internet, there are millions of web-sites. We are overloaded! The amount of information we can receive is overwhelming. We cannot process it. The choices are too much.

The same thing is true in the world of religion. There is a book listing more than ten thousand different religious denominations in our nation. We have enough choices to switch churches every two or three days if we wished. I've heard of church shopping, but that would be ridiculous!

Faced with choices, our age would like to have it all, to refuse to choose. Our culture prefers both/and to either/or. We resent the word "no" and take on more and more commitments, refusing to let go of old ones. But choices must be made, choices about where to focus energies, time, and behavior. Making a decision to do one thing closes out other possibilities. We may have the capability to receive hundreds of television channels, but we can only watch two or three at once. Kids may want to play on all teams, but they cannot play all the games on the same day. Maturity involves choice, either/or.

This is most keenly true in our faith. To choose the Christian life is to close out other possibilities. Can we say we are Christians without giving up contradictory behavior? Can we claim the name of Christ without giving up other claims? Are we willing to pick up the cross and choose to follow Christ alone?

Joshua understood that the most dangerous time for people of faith was not the time of hardship, but the time of affluence, the time of many choices. The people of Israel had come through a harrowing period of their history. After slavery in Egypt, they had wandered in a desert wilderness for an entire generation. Then, upon crossing the Jordan River, they had fought and won the land promised to them. Things were going to get easier now. They had arrived in the land flowing with milk and honey. All they needed would be provided, and this is the most dangerous time.

The comedian Dick Gregory once spoke about how the lack of commitment in American churches stems from freedom. As long as we are free to go to church on Sunday or not to go, there will not be much zeal. It takes oppression and hardship to generate religious fervor. To illustrate this, Gregory said that if a tank were put in front of the church door on Sundays to keep people away, attendance would increase significantly. As soon as you tell us we cannot go inside, we get fiery. Faced with freedom and choice, we become lethargic. Faced with oppression, we fight to the death.

So, ironically in a land of choice and religious freedom, we become lethargic. It is one of the symptoms of the decline of the church. Christians are becoming increasingly illiterate in our faith and apathetic. Christianity, a faith that requires our minds, hearts, bodies, and souls, becomes a hobby. Instead of integrating faith into the very core of our beings, we relegate it to the margins.

Joshua could imagine what would happen. Tolerating the gods of the Canaanites was tempting in a land of easy choice. Joshua knew how fickle his people could be. Why not accommodate all faiths, they asked? Why not put all truths and beliefs on an equal footing so that no one can take offense? Now that the people have arrived in the Promised Land, it would be easy to placate the local folks. Perhaps there would be benefits to serving other gods. The times were good . . . and dangerous. He urges the people not to give up their fire in the belly, their zeal for the Lord. He not only offers a choice in where they live, he offers them the choice of a god!

But Joshua calls them to choose Yahweh alone, the God who led them out of bondage into freedom and to the Promised Land. Likewise, to be a Christian means to put Christ first, and not to worship anything or anybody else. It means sacrificing many options. Christianity cannot be practiced on the edges of our lives, but only at the center. God wants converts, not adherents. When you say yes to God, you have to say no to something else. Jesus pressed hard decisions on would-be disciples. He tested the depth of conviction or shallowness of adhesion. When the rich young man was told, "Go, sell all you have, and follow me," his adherence to Jesus quickly dried up.

What will be our choice concerning our commitment to God? How shall we respond to God's goodness to us? Shall we be loyal to the God whose love is steadfast toward us? More money was spent on lotteries last year than was given to charities. What god *do* we serve?! In fact, far more money was spent on tickets to sporting events than was given for the work of God. Are we carrying any idols? In this congregation, one-sixth of the pledging families gave more than half of the church's total income.

It is the time of year for choosing financial stewardship. We have another choice to make. How shall we respond to God's grace and steadfast care? Shall we give sacrificially? Can we tie our giving to a proportion of our income? The choice we are making involves more than money. Which God do we serve? "Choose, this day, whom you will serve," says Joshua to the Israelites and to us. As for me and my household, we will serve the Lord. Our family's giving for next year will exceed $4500. Sadly, I am told that would make us one of the top nine givers of the church. That should not be. What will you do for the church of Jesus Christ in this place? You have choices to make. We hope you will prayerfully consider your pledge and choose whom you will serve.

As for me and my house, we will serve the Lord. How about you?

WHEN GOD'S BACK IS TURNED
Exodus 32:1–14; Matthew 22:1–14

Robert Richardson

As any parent knows, turning your back on young children can be risky. The telephone rings or there's a knock at the door, and you answer it. You are distracted, your back is turned, and the children sense that they're free to be children, free to do what they want.

Truth be told, of course, it is not only children who look for signals that an authority is distracted, leaving open an opportunity to get away with something. In fact, in the biblical texts read today, we hear about people who have discerned the signs that God was distracted, that God's back was turned to them. As such they were free to do as they desired.

In Exodus, Moses has been spending a great deal of time up on the mountain in the presence of God. God and Moses have been busy getting straight all the rules and ordinances by which the people are to live. Moses has made a number of trips up the mountain to receive further amplification and instruction. But this time, he has stayed too long. The people encamped below have grown weary of the wait. The silence and absence cause them to assume God's back is turned, and it is time to take matters into their own hands.

In Matthew, Jesus tells a tale about a king who wants to throw a wedding feast for his son. All the preparations were made and the guests invited. When it came time for the feast, the king sent out servants to announce all was ready. But since the king sent servants and did not go himself, those who heard the invitation from the servants assumed the king's back was turned, that he was occupied elsewhere and that those who had been invited were all free to do whatever they desired, which meant they did not go to the feast.

Jesus says the kingdom of heaven is like this, and if so, it means that the kingdom is a party to which everyone is invited, both good and bad. The invitation is given freely, but it is also an invitation that can be ignored. And if that decision is made, if we choose not to come to the feast, we are passed over and our seat is just as freely given to someone else, while we are left on the outside. The feast, the kingdom of God, goes on with or without us. When the people in the wilderness choose to turn away from God and to make and worship a golden calf, that did not mean that God was prevented from continuing to act in history, indeed, even in their very lives. God will continue to be active in the world with or without our consent.

But let's not get too complacent. You and I have made a decision to accept the king's invitation. Look at us: we have come to the party. And just because we are in the door does not mean that we have it made. Remember that poor sap in Jesus' parable? He showed up, but in thinking the king's back was turned, he did not put on a wedding garment. Therefore he was not merely tossed out into the street with those who had not come but instead was "cast into the outer darkness, where people weep and gnash their teeth." We had better keep an eye on this one, because we don't want to suffer a similar fate. Jesus' words are a clear indication that a favored position can be lost, especially if we live as though God's back is turned. Woe to the complacent! They can lose their seats in the kingdom.

A man named Clarence Jordan lived and worked in southern Georgia. He was an active member of his church, who taught Sunday school, preached an occasional sermon to fill in for his minister, and made a tithe to the church. He was a "pillar" in his church. And he took these words of Jesus to heart. He believed he had been invited to God's party, and he chose to respond. But Clarence also believed that just because he was in the party did not mean he could stay. He did not remain complacent and risk losing his seat.

Clarence began to go out into the rural areas around his church. Like the king in the parable, he invited any and all to come and work on his nearby farm. Soon the word got out and poor people, many without skills or shelter, began to arrive seeking work. It was not long until he was stretched to the limit and having a hard time maintaining his farm and caring for all those who had come to him seeking work and assistance in their lives. Needless to say, the neighbors were angry about this development taking place in their neighborhood.

As a man of strong Christian conviction, Clarence appealed to his church: "Let's join together to help our neighbors." One by one, the people of his church turned their backs on him. They demanded that he leave the church membership.

One person who came to work with Clarence was a fellow by the name of Millard Fuller. He began an organization that today is known as Habitat for Humanity, which builds homes along with the impoverished people who desire affordable housing. If you don't know about this ministry, you'll probably hear more from our Mission Committee. We are currently exploring a partnership with that organization, and doing what we can to assist them in their work.

As for Clarence Jordan's church, well, no one talks of it any more. I wonder if they were tossed out of heaven's party? They acted as if God's back was turned. They refused to help their neighbors in a time of need. They did not put on an appropriate wedding garment, and they might have been thrown out of the heavenly banquet as a result.

It's a challenging word that we hear from scripture today. What are you and I to make of it? Here we are, seated at the party of God's kingdom. We have responded to the invitation of the King and have made our way to the feast. We have come through the door and taken a seat at the table.

But the story makes us wonder if we are sitting here in the wrong clothes. Yes, everyone is invited, both the good and bad. All are welcome. It is a "come as you are" party. But once we come inside, we cannot stay as we came if we want to stay. The wedding garment must be put on. This parable haunts me. What if we are inside the door, sitting at the table but remaining just the way we arrived? What if the joyful apparel of the gospel is neatly folded and tucked away untouched in the closet?

What is this wedding garment we are required to wear if we want to stay? Nothing less than Christ. "Put on," as Paul says to the Romans, "the Lord Jesus Christ."

Yes, we have responded and we are at the feast. But have we put on the Lord Jesus Christ? Is there a discernible difference in our lives because we are here? Have we put on, as Paul implores the Colossians, compassion and kindness, lowliness, meekness, patience, love? Is the peace of Christ ruling our hearts, or are we ruled by concerns merely for ourselves and our institution? Are we concerned about the witness and work of our congregation, or is it a chore to listen to facts about our church's troubling financial situation because we have resolved to let other people do something about it? Do we do everything in the name of the Lord Jesus, or do we do it in our name? Have we put on the Lord Jesus Christ, or do we sit at the banquet in the same old clothes, hoping not to get thrown out because it looks like the king's back is turned?

The good news is that, all signs to the contrary, God's back is never turned. God saw what the people did at the base of the mountain, and God resolved to breathe hot wrath and consume them from the face of the earth. Those who skipped out of the feast found their city burned and themselves destroyed. And the one who came dressed inappropriately was cast out into the outer darkness. As the people of Clarence Jordan's church discovered, God's back was never turned on them, and God's back is never turned on us.

Have we put on our wedding garments? Have we put on the Lord Jesus Christ? Is Christ the head of this Church? Those are the questions that emerge from our texts.

If the answers to those questions are no, the outcome is bleak and the punishment harsh. But all of this is good news, because the invitation continues to be voiced. It is extended to us even yet today. The good news is that we matter to God, and God wants us at the feast and will stop at nothing to get us in the door and to get our clothes changed.

How does one respond to God's invitation? The possibilities and the opportunities are endless. It includes increasing our gifts to further the work of God's kingdom, especially when that opportunity comes your way in a few weeks on Stewardship Sunday. It includes consistent attendance at worship, and sharing your excitement about our church with friends whom you could invite to join you here. On Sunday morning, how about coming not only for worship but to one of our weekly adult education classes? We have two—wouldn't it be great to have to start some more? How about saying yes to the Nominating Committee when they call? Or volunteering to serve on a committee, visit our elderly and homebound, teach church school, compile the monthly newsletter, serve as an usher or acolyte, or go with us to the life center. We can live in such way, like Clarence Jordan, that the whole neighborhood begins to sit up and take notice that we have put on a new, joyous, and wondrous life.

So I invite each one of you to put on your wedding garment, and I charge us as a congregation to put on the Lord Jesus Christ. He has loved us enough to include us in his joyful celebration. For our part, we will strive to remain at the wondrous feast of God, and we will trust the grace and mercy of God that has gathered us here.

INTERPRETING OUR
GLOBAL RESPONSIBILITY
AND CONGREGATIONAL MISSION

DON'T TOUCH THE CHICKEN UNTIL WE SEE IF THEY ARE HUNGRY
Acts 4:32–35

Virginia Miner

When we were young, my brother and sister and I would be fascinated watching cars slip and slide on the snowy dirt road on the steep hill next to our house. Neighbors driving home during a snowstorm would build up speed on the highway, turn right onto the dirt road, and race up the hill hoping to maintain the necessary momentum to reach the top. From our window seat, we would cheer for those who succeeded and groan for those who landed in the ditch. Then we would run downstairs to find Dad already heading out to get the tractor to pull them out and my mother pulling out more plates to set on the table.

When these snowy mishaps created the possibility of unexpected guests at the table, we often heard Mom say, "Don't touch the chicken until we see if they are hungry." Some families call this F.H.B. (Family Hold Back), but in our house it was called "Don't touch the chicken!" (even if it was spaghetti). Because of this, a meal for five often fed seven or eight, and no one went hungry. We met most of our neighbors for the first time at these spontaneous meals, sharing what we had. While they ate, my father would pull their cars out of the ditch, and then we would all wait for the township plow to pass by, spraying ashes all over the ice.

This process of stretching the family meal taught us children two key spiritual lessons. First, we gained a healthy belief in the miracles of Jesus. Watching Mom feed many with a little, the feeding of the five thousand did not seem all that impossible to us! Second, we learned the difference between giving and sharing, the contrast between a condescending handout and the joyful gathering of neighbors around the table to share what we had.

In Acts 4:32–37, the writer says that the first Christians were one in mind and heart. What is even more amazing, they claimed for themselves no personal possessions but shared with one another everything they had. With a new faith came also a new way of life with an emphasis on sharing more than giving. This wasn't about handouts; it was about pulling together resources so all could have what was needed. Need was defined by what was required in order to go into the world and tell the good news of Jesus' death and resurrection, and this mission of their community called forth a method to meet their needs. Those who had resources shared what they had so all could serve the call of Christ.

Indeed, there is a difference between giving and sharing. Perhaps this is what the early church knew as it began its life together. They knew that sharing was kinder than giving. They knew that sharing was not a means for controlling others but a means for providing help for those in need.

This distinction between giving and sharing really came home to me when I visited Nicaragua on a Witness for Peace trip in 1987. Before we arrived in Managua, we were instructed in cultural sensitivity. This sensitivity training reminded me of preparations for visiting my great aunt Jenny. My parents always went over the dos and don'ts of how to be polite in her presence. Rules like "Don't jump on the sofa," "Don't take food unless offered," and "Speak loudly and clearly so she can hear you" were all in "The Handbook of Instruction for Visits to Older Relatives."

For the mission trip to Nicaragua, we were instructed not to give things away impulsively. Our ability to give stuff (T-shirts, pens, cameras, and so on) so far overwhelmed the rural person's ability to return the favor that it would be humiliating. In truth, such inequity would be embarrassing in any culture. Just the contents in my backpack exceeded the value of some of the homes in which I stayed. In the face of such poverty, one's first instinct is to give everything away, but doing so only creates a greater separation from the people one wants to get to know.

So the rule was, we could share anything with our hosts that we could also use with them. The distinction was important. For example, I could leave a deck of playing cards with the children in my host's home if I played cards with them. The key here was to give something of ourselves along with our possessions. This meant that I could leave behind my Spanish-English dictionary, because it was the key to our communication during my three-day visit. It wasn't just a "thing," it was part of me and part of what we had shared together. Neither the guests nor the hosts could change the circumstances of our birth, but we could seek to meet as equals in the name of Christ and work toward sharing the means necessary for mission, for God's work of justice and peace.

The early Christians understood this difference well. In our passage in

Acts 4, we see a good example of a Christian community whose goal was not so much to give to those in need but rather to share the resources needed to support those who were seeking to tell the good news. However, it has been said that the greatest threat is a good example. Perhaps this is why this Acts passage has always caused some controversy. Could we live in a world where "no one claimed ownership of private possessions, but everything they owned was held in common?" Could we live in a world that had a passion for sharing? The Greek word here (*koina*), which is translated "shared," is the same that is at the root of *koinonia*, which means "community." Could it be that the essence of any community is its ability to share?

This notion of community built on sharing is threatening because we live in a culture that prefers to collect rather than to share. I once was invited to a bridal shower. Following the meal, the bride began the lengthy process of opening all her gifts. Among the first gifts was an electric can opener. How exciting! Several minutes later she unwrapped a second electric can opener and then a third. Finally, near the end of the gifts, came yet a fourth electric can opener. Nearly at a loss for words, the bride exclaimed, "Well, this is good; I would simply die without my electric can opener." Showing great restraint, I muttered to myself, "No, but you might die without any cans to open." I left the shower with the impression that she might very well keep all four can openers. What I found even more discouraging was that she couldn't imagine life with without one. I hope her neighbors shared in her abundance.

We often live as people hungry to collect possessions and then afraid of losing them. But these things are not ours to possess in the first place. All we have comes from God and is really only ours on loan. We forget that.

Inspired one day by a conversation with a man concerned about whether the social security system would still have money when he retired, I wrote this poem:

> To those who only want
> there to be enough
> when it is their turn.
> How much
> is enough?

When you have nothing, how much is enough? When you have everything, how much is enough? Perhaps it is not a question of how much but a question of how well. How well do we use what is entrusted to us by God for the benefit of those with whom we share this planet?

Some argue the early Christians were already so preoccupied with heaven that they cared nothing for this world so it was easier for them to live together sharing their possessions. However, I think the opposite is true. If it were easy, everybody would do it. Sharing is not about how much we throw into the common pot—it is about how we involve ourselves in the needs of others.

Once on a retreat, a group of twelve of us played a game where we were to imagine that all of us were about to be taken away to a deserted island. The idea was that we were all going to be together, but each of us could only take one personal item. The question was, what would you take? After a little time to think about this question, we all reported back on our choices.

I have played this game several times with several different groups, but only once did a group work together so that the community would have twelve different, necessary items for the good of the whole. Every other time, each person did an independent thing, and the group ended up with six Bibles, one toothbrush, and a lot of photographs. It isn't a simple task to live together with a concern for the needs of all. It requires a change in how we think before we can change how we act. It requires a focus on a common goal.

Perhaps the first Christians were already familiar with a better way to use life's resources. The principle of *tsedakah* in Jewish law means helping those in need fulfill their potential. There are eight degrees in the giving of tsedakah:

1. Those who give grudgingly, reluctantly, or with regret.
2. Those who give less than is fitting, but give graciously.
3. Those who give what is fitting, but only after being asked.
4. Those who give before being asked.
5. Those who give without knowing to whom, although the recipients know the identity of the donors.
6. Those who give without making their identity known to the recipients.
7. Those who give without knowing to whom and neither do the recipients know from whom they receive.
8. Those who help others by giving a gift or loan, or by making them business partners or finding them employment, thereby helping them dispense aid to others. As Scripture says, "you shall strengthen him, be he stranger or settler, he shall live with you (Leviticus 23:35)." This means strengthening them in such a manner that falling into want is prevented.[1]

As we share what God has given us, we empower others to fulfill the image of God within them. We give strength to each other to witness to the God who has made us stewards of the world that is the Lord's so that no one leaves the table hungry. May we be worthy of such a trust.

IF THERE ISN'T ENOUGH TO GO AROUND
Matthew 14:13–21

William G. Carter

Nobody could blame the disciples for their concern. It had been a long and exhausting day. People from all over the countryside had followed Jesus with their aches and pains. Rather than retreat or rest, Jesus stayed there, the Gospel of Matthew tells us, and saved all of them, one at a time.

Meanwhile his twelve followers were overwhelmed by the need. It was getting late, and all they could see was a long line of needy people who would not go away. "Lord," they said, "there isn't enough food to go around. Send these people away so they can get something to eat."

Here is a story we can understand. The needs of the world are overwhelming. What can we do? Where would we start? Our resources are so limited and the needs are so great. A huge number of the world's people are starving for food. Many more are hungry for something more.

A man named Kevin recently returned from a trip to Ethiopia. His church is building a relationship with a congregation in Ethiopia, and he went to the country to meet people in the church. He returned shocked by the hunger in Addis Ababa. In the capital city, there is a sea of humanity begging for money or food. Most beggars are little children. The guide said, "Stay away from them and watch out for pickpockets."

At one point, someone bumped into Kevin and stuck a hand in his pocket. Kevin grabbed the person's wrist and started yelling at him. The man screamed back. They did not understand one another. Kevin let him go. A few minutes later, Kevin realized he was missing some coins from his other pocket. The total value was about two American dollars, but it made him angry. He caught up with his fellow travelers, his hands now guarding his pockets.

Meanwhile one hand after another reached out for help. "Money, mister? Mister, some money? Money please?"

After a few blocks of that, Kevin's anger had subsided. What are a couple of bucks when so many people have so little? Kevin said, "I could be a millionaire and give everything away to those people, and it would not make a dent in their situation."

What do you do? The need is so great. The resources are so few. There wasn't enough to go around. Do you know how that feels?

Your church knows how it feels. Every November, the leaders of this congregation sharpen their pencils and work on the budget. We want to glorify God by providing a full range of programs, reaching out to the needy, and meeting some established obligations. And when we meet to prepare the next year's budget, there is always a shadow of disappointment over the group. We never seem to have enough money to do the things God calls us to do.

The needs are great. We seem to have so little. We can understand this story about a multitude of hungry people who are approached with a couple of fish and five loaves of bread. The resources never seem to stretch far enough. Nobody is surprised to hear the disciples say, "Lord, send them away."

According to the Gospel of Matthew, however, Jesus did not let his fishermen off the hook. As surely as this story of feeding the multitude is about Jesus, the founder of the feast, it is also a story about his twelve disciples. When the Twelve said, "Lord, get rid of this crowd," he replied, "You give them something to eat!" Now that's a striking aspect to this story. Jesus does not turn stones into loaves of bread to feed the crowd. Instead he demands that his followers pitch in and give what they have. The Gospel of Matthew insists the disciples gave their own bread and fish. There is no mention of a young boy who offers his lunch; that's in the Gospel of John. This is Matthew, and in Matthew, Jesus says, "You give them something to eat."

They respond, "All we have are five loaves and a couple of fish." So he asks for it. They give Jesus everything they possess. He thanks God for it. He breaks the bread. And he gives them back the bread in order for them to give it away to others. After the crowds eat their fill, they take up the leftovers.

By the way, did you hear how many baskets were left over? There were twelve baskets of bread left! That's one for each disciple. Isn't that something? They gave everything to Jesus. He blessed it, broke it, gave it back to be given away. In the economy of God, the disciples who gave everything to the Lord received everything they needed in return.

Do you suppose God still works like that? We hope so. We would like to think we could give everything to God and get all we need in return. Unfortunately such a great economy breaks down somehow. Our hearts may be convinced of the great needs of the church or the world, but we grow afraid. The fists clench shut. The purse closes. The wallet snaps shut. It takes a direct intervention to change us.

It reminds me of the preacher who was leading the people in worship one day. It was time for the weekly offering and she said, "I want all of you to stand up for a minute." Everybody stood. Then she said, "I want all of you to lean forward, grab the wallet or purse of the person in front of you, and give as you always wanted to, but never had the chance." That would be fun, wouldn't it? And giving ought to be fun!

But the opposite of generosity is fear. We look at what little we have, and we think of the reasons why we can't help. D. H. Lawrence tells a story about a family with a boy and two little girls. They lived in a nice house with a garden. Yet the family felt an anxiety: there was never enough money. Both mother and father had small incomes, but they didn't have enough to reach the social position they desired. The father pursued business leads that never materialized. The mother tried to earn more money, but her failures etched deep lines into her face.

In time, their home became haunted with the unspoken phrase, "There must be more money." No one ever said it aloud, least of all the children. But the words filled the home, especially when expensive toys filled the nursery.

> Behind the shining modern rocking-horse, behind the smart doll's-house, a voice would start whispering: "There *must* be more money! There *must* be more money!" The children could hear it all the time, though nobody said it aloud. And the children would stop playing, to listen for a moment. They would look into each other's eyes, to see if they had all heard. And each one saw in the eyes of the other two that they too had heard. "There *must* be more money! There *must* be more money! . . ."
>
> Yet nobody ever said it aloud. The whisper was everywhere, and therefore no one spoke it. Just as no one ever says: "We are breathing!" in spite of the fact that breath is coming and going all the time.[1]

Did you ever hear that haunting whisper in your home? I'm talking about that quiet voice that says, "There must be more money." Meanwhile, money keeps coming and going all the time.

Jesus intervenes by saying, "You give them something to eat. You teach your neighbors how to pray. You send out missionaries to address the world's aches and pains. You sing the hymns that praise God's name. You give your money to further the work of the church."

Usually our first response is to look down and say, "We don't have what it takes," or "We don't have the ability," or "We don't have the money." Then to ease our consciences, we drive off to the Mammon Warehouse and buy a few things we don't need.

It strikes me that Jesus takes whatever his disciples give him, in this case, two fish and five loaves. After he thanks God, he breaks what they give him, and says, "Now, give it away." He broke their gifts of bread. They could no longer hold them, hoard them, keep them, preserve them, or protect them. Instead they were broken, so that everybody could have a piece.

Oh, if we could only dare to let that happen! We're so afraid there isn't going to be enough food or money or whatever else to go around. So we start stockpiling it. Or we use more than our share. You've heard statistics like that. The United States has only 5.6 percent of the world's population. Yet we consume 42 percent of the world's aluminum, 33 percent of the world's copper, 44 percent of the world's coal, 33 percent of the world's petroleum, and 63 percent of the world's natural gases.[2]

Why do we do it? Because we are afraid there isn't going to be enough to go around. Oh, if God would only give us new eyes, that we could see our circumstances in relation to the needs of the world! Oh, if God would only give us new hearts, so we could trust God to take our offerings and do something beautiful with them! Oh, if God would only take our prized possessions and break them into something new, so that the hungry would be fed and the good news would be proclaimed!

The more I think about it, the more I realize stewardship is a matter of conversion. Those of us in the Western world live with the myth of scarcity, even though the world is filled with signs of God's abundant generosity. We need to be converted, so we might become generous just like God. That is especially true for those of us who have so much, yet are convinced we have so little. Nothing short of a conversion would do.

A minister worked as an interim pastor of a church where people are accustomed to doing the same thing every week. The members of that church have a lot of customs and traditions, and they don't like anybody disrupting them. One custom has been to put a loaf of bread on the communion plate every week.

They do not celebrate the Lord's Supper every week, but they have a symbol of the sacrament. If you think that would be expensive or wasteful to have an unused loaf of bread on the communion table every week, don't worry. They use the same loaf. It is a large unsliced loaf of Italian bread covered with polyurethane. So they use the same bread over and over again. One Sunday my friend was leading the people in communion. He lifted the ceremonial loaf of bread, said, "Take, eat, this is my body." Then he cracked it open and ripped it apart.

There was a collective gasp in the congregation. Then it was absolutely silent as he continued to break the bread into large chunks to place on the communion trays. It took a few minutes for people to realize my friend had switched the polyurethane bread with a real loaf. Afterward, someone said, "You really had us going there for a minute. We thought you actually broke our communion bread."

The minister said, "Don't you understand? If it isn't broken, it can't be shared."

WHAT WE HAVE KNOWN IN THIS PLACE
1 Thessalonians 1:1–10

George Chorba

I don't know if you sort through the day's mail as I do, but over time I've developed a system, and it may be a familiar one. The Christmas catalogs that begin arriving with the last hint of summer go into one pile. Letters with those computerized mailing labels go into another, and anything addressed "occupant" is put into the circular file. This is particularly true for anything stamped "Urgent! You may be a winner. Open immediately." With all due haste, I neatly fold that envelope into the shape of a paper airplane, and urgently send it toward the basket.

The ones I keep to be opened immediately, however, are those addressed to me personally. But even then, you can be fooled. A friend showed me a thank-you letter he'd received after sending a political contribution. Because his gift had been accompanied by his business letterhead, he was addressed in five different places as "Dear Mr. Corporation." So much for the personal touch! I was assured that the candidate won't be receiving the follow-up gift that was requested—at least not from "Mr. Corporation."

There could not be a greater contrast between this falsely personal touch and the two deeply and genuinely personal letters Paul writes to the Thessalonian Christians. Paul knows the Thessalonians, and his words to them are truly personal. He begins with the affectionate words that have shaped the Christian community in all times and places: "Grace to you and peace." And he continues with what he knows of them personally, saying, "I give thanks to God for all of you, remembering in my prayers your work of faith, your labor of love, and your steadfastness of hope in our Lord Jesus Christ." And after two letters, containing eight chapters, in which he pours out his gratitude for all they have meant to him, he signs the letters, saying, "I, Paul write this greeting with my own hand. This is the mark in every letter of mine; it is the way I write. The grace of our Lord Jesus Christ be with you all."

"It is the way I write to you . . . for your work of faith, your labor of love, and your steadfastness of hope in our Lord," and these personal letters of Paul have been filed in the heart of the Christian community for nearly two thousand years now. About two months ago I opened an envelope from a recent new member of our church, and what they wrote sent me on a memory search through these ancient letters of Paul. I was reminded so much of Paul's profound gratitude for the Thessalonian church. The letter I opened was written by hand. "Dear George," it began, "I had become estranged from the church that was my solace and refuge about 25 years ago. Over time," the letter continued, "I tried many times to reconcile myself to the church, but it did not work out. I was mentioning this at lunch one day and several friends said I must come here to the crossroads. One Sunday I found myself entering the church. I found a corner where I sat down, and there was an overwhelming feeling of having come home. This feeling has not left me, and I only hope I can give back in some way the thankfulness of finding this church and the loving people I have come to know here. God bless and be with you."

As I read that letter, grace and peace seemed to flood my office on that late summer morning; the grace and peace of coming home to a community shaped by your work of faith, your labor of love, and your steadfast hope in the Lord. And so today, I want to speak with you for a few minutes about that power, about the power of what we have known in this place. A power that has made you an example to other believers in an area at least as large as Macedonia and Achaia combined.

So today, I, like Paul, give thanks to God for "your work of faith." Notice that Paul calls it a "work of faith," not "a gift of faith." Faith begins as a gift, of course, but faith becomes worthy of gratitude when the gift is transformed into action, when our faith presses us to risk who we are and what we have on behalf of others. This is the work of faith.

Twenty-five years ago, no one in Morris County had faith in minority families who lived in public housing, except the people of this church. In those days, minority families were caught in a vise. On the one hand, as their incomes rose by working two and three jobs simultaneously, they were routinely rewarded for this hard work with eviction notices, by being thrown out of their homes. On the other hand, they were blocked by the banks from securing mortgages to buy their own homes. No one would lend them money. They were considered very bad risks, and no one had faith in them.

This church looked at the small endowment we had and decided to risk all of it, if larger congregations around us with sizable endowments would commit a small portion of what they had. Now, whether it was out of embarrassment or because of faith in us, I don't know, but five other congregations did just that. And so the Morris Housing Investment Fund was formed to grant second mortgages to these families, if a bank could be found to stand in first position on the loans. One small bank in Morristown finally agreed, and over the next fifteen years, that act of faith has resulted in hundreds of mortgages with such a negligible default rate that every other bank in the county rewrote their lending policies. So, because this congregation risked its entire endowment, the banking community of Morris County changed its course and minority families had access to the same kind of trust everyone else enjoyed. That is the work of faith.

Twenty years ago, no one I knew in this area had any faith that retarded young people could be productive and support themselves. It was fair to say they were seen as victims of circumstance, rather than capable, contributing members of society. They were held in special education classes until they were twenty-one, and then they were sent home. As one educator told us: yes, they were sent home to watch television for the rest of their lives. But one member of this church knew better, and so the resources and resourcefulness of our church were gathered to create the first sheltered workshop in the state. We rented a vacant building over in Madison and begged equipment to furnish it from local corporations, hired a staff, provided volunteers, and then sought companies who would bring work to the center for these young people to do. At the end of one week of operation, they got the first paychecks they had received in their lives, and I wish you could have seen their faces. They also got the training they needed to secure jobs outside the center, and then the State of New Jersey began looking into what was going on here. In three years we were able to close that center because legislation was passed to create sheltered workshops in every county, based on the model we created right here. One person's vision—embraced by the people of faith in this place—and these wonderful young people had the future they deserved. The work of faith.

And your labor of love. You know, of course, that we baptize infants and children in this place because there is no more precious gift God gives to us than these children. We place the mark of faith upon their foreheads and promise to love them as our own. They are a tremendous joy to us. Every one of them. But you also know there are children born with a different mark upon their lives. For many of them, their parents are children themselves. And unfortunately they are parents who are homeless and unable or unwilling to care for these infants.

Well, six years ago you made a home for those infants down in Newark so they didn't have to linger on the maternity floor of Newark's hospitals. You multiplied a small gift that had been given to you by the work of your hands and turned it into a major grant to make that place safe and secure. Then you searched your own homes for cribs and strollers and playpens. You gathered blankets, planted bulbs, and built a terrace from the bricks we took up from the front of our church. And for the last six years of her life, a woman of our church knit feverishly every day she could, and there was a steady flow of booties and blankets and bonnets, which we carried down to that home for infants, infants we may never know or be able to name. Your labor of love.

And so, I give thanks to God for all of you who have made this possible, beginning what no one else would begin and supporting it significantly every year since. Your steadfast hope in Jesus Christ continues to make a difference in the life of everyone who comes into this place. The daughter of our oldest living member speaks for her mother when she writes:

> The impact of this church's life for my mother, Elizabeth, has to be the wonderful birthday tributes when she turned 95 and 96 and, then, 97. When everyone stood to sing "Happy Birthday," it was like the warmth from the light of all those candles which would have been on a birthday cake, and it gave a glow to her and her family that will never go out. She had always taken us to church—wherever we were in all of her 39 moves in an army life, sometimes when the congregation was smaller than the choir! And it has been a marvelous happening that her last church has given her so much love. Every Sunday it is a joy for me to walk through the church doors, to be greeted so warmly, to anticipate the beautiful music and flowers, and experience the warmth and love in this church. It is always the same wonderful event. [signed] A grateful daughter

Steadfast hope in Jesus Christ is not an accident of good fortune. It is an event, an event you can anticipate because of what you have wanted this church to be, for yourself and for everyone who comes here. Paul calls it an exemplary life, not because you think of yourselves as an example to others, but because that is the way others see you. Your faith, he says, your faith has become known to others.

COME AND SEE
John 1:43–51

Paul Debenport

Nazareth? "Can anything good come out of Nazareth?"

When Philip told his friend Nathanael that he had found the longed-for Messiah, Nathanael reacted as so many others would respond to Jesus later—with skeptical, but understandable, doubt.

"Can anything good come out of Nazareth?"

Of course, the one fact we know about Nathanael is that he was from Cana, a rival town about ten miles from Nazareth. So perhaps Nathanael's sarcastic question was simply the common putdown of the nearby town, just as the people of Dallas used to mock my native town, Fort Worth, asking, "Can anything good come out of Cowtown?"

Maybe Nathanael was just being flippant. But maybe not. Maybe there was something deeper under his skeptical retort. Perhaps old Nathanael had simply seen too much of life to even begin to hope that the age-old promise of God might actually be fulfilled in his lifetime. Perhaps he was simply guarding himself against another letdown, another disappointment, calling the grapes sour before even tasting them. After all, then as now, false messiahs were a dime a dozen.

Did his friend, Philip, really expect Nathanael to be so naïve? So quick to believe? So ready to follow? But Philip persisted. "Come and see," he invited. The fact that Nathanael went shows that, beneath his armor of understandable doubt, there was still a speck of hope, enough hope, at least, to be willing to come and see.[1]

On this Stewardship Sunday, when we are being invited to graciously, generously, and gratefully commit a significant portion of our personal financial resources to the work of Christ through this church, the connection with this passage is the understandable question that this stewardship invitation raises in our minds: Albuquerque? Can anything good come out of First Presbyterian Church, Albuquerque?

"Come and see!"

Come and see a family of faith that takes God's word and Christ's mission seriously, lovingly, and responsibly.

Come and see church school classes, women's circles, covenant groups studying scripture with minds as well as hearts engaged, better to discern God's good word, and so as not to abuse God's word with toxic faith and spurious doctrines. But come and see minds and hearts engaged responsibly with God and God's word.

Come and see a family of faith struggling to be "doers of the word and not hearers only."

Come and see adults, youth, and children actively serving others as Christ has served us—right here in Albuquerque, in our country, and around the world.

Come and see Habitat for Humanity houses being built, meals served to homeless families, spiritual counseling and prayers shared with strangers as well as members.

Come and see desperate people, up to five a day, who see our soaring cross and seek all kinds of help, from a meal to a tank of gas to prayers and pastoral counseling and pastoral calls to their daughters and sons and parents in our nearby hospitals. Come and see how Christ is proclaimed as Messiah through our actions as well as our words.

Come and see a family of faith where women and men, young and old, married and single, widowed and divorced, sick and well, rich and poor and in-between are valued, empowered as equal members of this church family.

Come and see a family of faith actively reaching to include and value and love children and youth. See the biblically grounded, theologically sound church school classes and Vacation Bible School.

Come and see a community proactively helping children and youth actually enjoy worship, helping children be able both to learn from worship and to offer their spiritual gifts in worship.

Come and see a church where maturity and age are valued as treasured members of the church family. Come and see an active, vital senior league, and seniors serving on every committee and board of the church. Come and see a well-governed church, with responsible, representative leaders of all ages.

"Can anything good come out of First Presbyterian Church, Albuquerque?"

Come and see the revitalized intergenerational happening at "Wednesday Night Live," where everything from parenting classes to spiritual development classes to groups just relaxing together playing bridge and board games are full of adults, growing in faith and in fellowship. Our children and youth are there, too, gathering for everything from Bible study to dance, to choir, to art, to fun and fellowship. Come and see the love and grace of Jesus Christ coming alive at "Wednesday Night Live."

Come and see ministries of care, compassion, and spiritual support. See the Deacons calling on, praying with, and caring for the scores of homebound, hospitalized, and nursing-home–bound members of this church. Come and see the pastors, elders, and deacons going into the community to serve communion and pray with the sick, the infirm, the dying, and all those who can no longer come here.

Come and see, or in this case, come and hear. Hear the glory of God being proclaimed more powerfully than ever through our growing choirs. Come and hear. Let yourselves be inspired by angels ascending and descending in worship. Come and see, too, the fellowship groups, who have gone deeper with each other when crisis and tragedy have hit. Come and see them gathering in hospital chapels and homes to pray together and support each other through their times of crisis.

Nathanael, come and see the love and grace and healing of Jesus Christ being lived each and every day, 365 days of the year.

Angels, ascending and descending.

Can anything good come out of First Presbyterian Church, Albuquerque? Come and see. Believe and recommit.

All our ministries happen with great dedication and commitment by you, the members of this church. Your time, your prayers, your skills, and your money are the resources that God uses to be Christ's angels ascending and descending between heaven and this particular part of earth.

In proclaiming this passage on Stewardship Sunday, I am also thinking of another understandable, Nathanael-like question that we silently ask ourselves this time of year: "A bigger budget? Can anything good come out of a bigger budget?"

Come and see. Come and see how an active church family, with more people and groups served by our buildings and ministries just costs more.

Come and see how what used to be thirty-dollar repair bills are now hundred- and even thousand-dollar repair bills, just as in our homes.

Come and see how increased ministry means increased hours of heating and air-conditioning and lighting.

Come and see how more youth and children going to more camps and conferences and retreats for their spiritual growth and development requires more budget support.

Come and see the practical concerns, like how Christian Education curricula cost more, choir anthems more, organ tuning more and all the other things we usually just take for granted.

Come and see. Believe, and prayerfully make your recommitment decision. For if we respond like Nathanael, then, as Jesus promised, we too "will see greater things than these!"

SOMEONE IN THE CROWD
Luke 12:13–20

George Chorba

A number of years ago we embarked on a high-risk venture here at the church. It started when we received an unexpected gift from an anonymous donor. There were no strings on this gift; we could use it in any way we saw fit. At the time, it was one of the largest single gifts we had ever received, and it came as a kind of unexpected inheritance, along with the trust that it would be used well. In most churches, that kind of gift probably would have been added to the endowment, and that would be that.

But the high-risk venture we embarked on then was the decision to give this gift to people who didn't really need it. The week before Palm Sunday, the gift was converted to cash, placed in hundreds of small envelopes, and distributed to every single man, woman, and child who came to church on Palm Sunday and Easter. The note that accompanied each gift was very simple: "This is a gift for you. If you need this gift, it is yours. If you know someone who needs it more, it is your gift to give. Or you can multiply the gift by investing it with your time, talent, and energy, and we will harvest those multiplied gifts on the first Sunday in October."

The response was immediate and overwhelming. Vegetable gardens were planted, bird houses built, flower gardens were set, seedlings were sold, rag dolls were sewn, families pooled their gifts and held dinners, small stocks were purchased, baby-sitting services were started, and week by week those small gifts grew. On World Communion Sunday, we harvested here an embarrassment of riches. That anonymous gift had been multiplied fivefold, and we were able to build the first library ever at a small school in a countryside village of Kenya. Two of the students who poured over the first books they had ever held have now been educated in

America and have returned to Kenya as teachers. And so the gift continues to grow on and on into the future.

This is one picture of abundance, a gift multiplied and transformed into an open future we could not have envisioned. Our text for this morning offers another picture, though, one with a closed future. Someone in the crowd around Jesus says to him, "Tell my brother to divide the family inheritance with me." The emphasis here is not on the inheritance but on "me." Jesus tells the man, "I am not a judge or an arbitrator of greed . . . for your life does not consist in the abundance of possessions."

Then Jesus tells them a parable. "The land of a certain rich man produced abundantly. And he thought to himself, what should I do?" As the story develops, the rich man's abundance is hoarded greedily into barns, and the parable ends as his life does, tragically and without a future. Now I want to stop the parable there for just a moment and ask you to think about this rich man's abundance, to think about it as another form of high-risk venture, a venture where the risk is investing in oneself rather than in others.

I want to ask you to hold this man in your heart for a moment and try to see him as Jesus does. Not as a tyrant or an egomaniac but as a sadly foolish and isolated human being. Although we don't even know the man's name, it turns out we do know a great deal about him. He is careful. He is conservative. The parable tells us that. The parable also tells us that he lives for himself. He talks to himself. He plans for himself, and then he even congratulates himself.[1] It is a life of carefully constructed boundaries that all begin with the word "me" and end with the word "mine," sadly isolated in that sacred precinct of the self.

Jesus never calls the man selfish or says he is unjust, because nothing is ever taken from others that is not already his. What Jesus does point to is the sad isolation of a life that has no future, because the boundaries of his life are so tightly drawn. Jesus knows the inner workings, the secret heart of this rich man—and not just of the rich man but of all of us. Indeed, after telling the story of the rich man, Jesus turns to his disciples and names the secret worry and isolation of all of us, a kind of symbiosis where anxiety feeds on isolation, and isolation nourishes anxiety. It is a symbiosis that Jesus names when he asks, "Why do you worry and keep striving as this rich man does? Consider the birds of the air and the lilies of the field. Are you not of more value than they?" Jesus is not posing here as a poor man's psychoanalyst when he asks questions like this, but he does seem to know that the fast track to isolation is paved by anxiety, by what you and I worry about when we are alone.

And what Jesus offers is not a first-century variety of anxiety therapy but the image of a life so valued that God knows what we need before we even know what to ask. That is exactly what Jesus offered when he said, "I have come so that you might have life, and have it more abundantly"—a life where the boundaries between me and mine begin to loosen and the distinction between my abundance and yours begins to blur. It's not a self-less life but a self-giving one, because this value God has placed on your life is meant to be given away; it's meant to be invested in others and ulti-mately brought to harvest in a future that cannot be imagined or dreamed at the moment. And Jesus tells us this is life with a future. Your future and God's.

The last line of Brian Wren's marvelous contemporary hymn "There's a Spirit in the Air" puts it another way: "Live tomorrow's life today."[2] That's our business as a church. Helping others live God's future today. Once, in a church that can remain nameless, someone in the crowd at a coffee hour bent over a young boy and asked him, "What do you want to be when you grow up?" The boy's answer was "An adult!" Well, you can't define the future—or the future of the church, any better than that. We're in the busi-ness of growing adults, people whose lives have a future.

I want to leave you with two reasons why the stewardship of our abun-dance might be important to you. And the first of the reasons is that you and I have come to a church today where our lives are precious. Precious to God and to the people around you in these pews. And that isn't an idle claim I make. Several months ago I opened a note in the mail from a woman who is not a member of our church. She wrote to say, "I still can't believe the outpouring of affection and support that surrounded me when my husband died. I feel like I've inherited a whole circle of new friends in people I'd never known before. I'm still overwhelmed. And if it's sup-posed to be true that you only reap what you sow in this life, I can only tell you I never planted the seeds of this incredible abundance. But someone else must have."

Now there is one thing that I do know for certain, and that is the people who reached out to her and touched her so deeply would be embarrassed if you told them they had done anything extraordinary. Because they only reflected how much they feel valued by God and the people who have loved them in this church. All they did was give someone else what they have received in the first place. "Consider the birds of the air," Jesus said. "They neither sow nor do they reap, and yet God feeds them." That's how precious you are in this place. There is no means test to qualify you for this gift. It is God's, and God's alone to give. All we do is to invest it in others when God gives us that opportunity.

The other reason I want to mention for the stewardship of our abun-dance is that you and I have come to a place today where our business is investing in the future God has already prepared for us. Jesus called it "his kingdom." A kingdom where God provides what we need, and our job is to invest our abundance in people whose lives have a future. You see that future every time you come here.

Several years ago, one of our college students called me from his dormitory during his senior year. He had been one of those children we taught and loved and prayed for as he grew up in our church. What he called to tell me was how grateful he felt that we'd sent him each summer on our senior-high summer work projects. They had a real impact on his life, and now he wanted to do something like that on his own when he graduated. But he didn't know quite what it would be.

So we sent him to that village in Kenya to work in that library built through that high-risk venture so many years before, to work with the children in the school there. We sent him with a guitar and a bicycle and not much else really, except the money he would need for his room and board. He spent half a year there playing that guitar and helping children to read the books that we had sent them. We told him this was the church's mission. He told me he didn't feel worthy to be a missionary. I told him to let God worry about that. We knew what we were doing in sending him. And so he went. Since he has been back, he has dedicated his life to working with children who may never be able to read, but God has let him see that they, too, have a future and he wants to be part of it.

That is the kind of quiet miracle the stewardship of our abundance creates, with gifts that continue to grow through the years. We are so blessed. We really are. Because this is a place where every one of us can live tomorrow's life today . . . and so it is with a real sense of honor that I invite you to be part of that high-risk venture this year.

Notes

Introduction

1. Fred B. Craddock, *Preaching* (Nashville: Abingdon Press, 1985), 153–69.
2. Walter Brueggemann, "The Third World of Evangelical Imagination," in *Interpretation and Obedience: From Faithful Reading to Faithful Living* (Minneapolis: Fortress Press, 1991), 13.
3. Loren B. Mead, "Caught in the Financial Bind: Reflections on Clergy and Money," *Congregations* 23, no. 3 (July/August 1996): 3.
4. Thomas G. Long, "The Use of Scripture in Contemporary Preaching," *Interpretation* 44, no. 4 (October 1990): 351.
5. Fred B. Craddock, "Preaching about Giving Thanks: Giving God Thanks and Praise," in *Preaching In and Out of Season*, ed. Thomas G. Long and Neely Dixon McCarter (Louisville, Ky.: Westminster/John Knox Press, 1990), 121.
6. George Herbert, "Gratefulnesse," in *The English Poems of George Herbert* (Totowa, N.J.: Dent, Rowman, and Littlefield, 1978), 135–36.
7. Lesslie Newbigin, *The Gospel in a Pluralist Society* (Grand Rapids: Wm. B. Eerdmans Publishing Co., 1989), 227.

Good Circulation

1. Copyright by Thomas H. Troeger, 1997, used by permission.

Resources at the Ready

1. Fred B. Craddock, et al., *Preaching the New Common Lectionary, Year A after Pentecost* (Nashville: Abingdon Press, 1987), 271.

Grace and Grab

1. John Dominic Crossan, *In Parables: The Challenge of the Historical Jesus* (San Francisco: Harper & Row, 1973), 109.

2. Kenneth E. Bailey, *Poet and Peasant* (Grand Rapids: Wm. B. Eerdmans Publishing Co., 1976), 86–110.

The Heart of the Matter

1. Jacques Ellul, *Hope in Time of Abandonment* (New York: Seabury Press, 1973), 3.
2. *Ibid.*, 8.
3. *Ibid.*, 191.
4. Hans-Joachim Kraus, *Theology of the Psalms* (Minneapolis: Augsburg Publishing House, 1986), 145–46.

Whatever?

1. As quoted in *Weavings* 11, no. 4 (July/August 1996): 32–33.

Not as an Exaction

1. William Barclay, *The Letters to the Corinthians* (Philadelphia: Westminster Press, 1975), 259.
2. Mark Landfried, *This Service of Love* (Camp Hill, Pa.: Synod of the Trinity, 1978), 66–69.
3. Barclay, *Letters*, 259.
4. Landfried, *This Service*, 68.
5. Clarence Cave, *Think Piece 2* (New York: United Presbyterian Support Agency, 1975), 67.

Hilarious Giving

1. Parker J. Palmer, *The Active Life: Wisdom for Work, Creativity, and Caring* (San Francisco: HarperCollins, 1990), 124–25.
2. As quoted by Martin Marty, in his newsletter *Context*.
3. I am grateful to Donel McClellan for this story.

Marvelous Mammon

1. "GM's Outgoing Chairman to Get Boost in Pension," *Ministry of Money* newsletter, number 66, June 1990: 1–2.
2. Thomas G. Long, *The Gospel of Matthew* (Louisville, Ky.: Westminster John Knox Press, 1997), 74.

Don't Touch the Chicken Until
We See If They Are Hungry

1. An epitome of Maimonides' Eight Degrees of Tsedekah, Mishnah Torah, Gifts to the Needy, 10 (taken from *Guide My Feet, Prayers and Meditations for Our Children,* Marian Wright Edelman, p. 99).

If There Isn't Enough to Go Around

1. D. H. Lawrence, "The Rocking-Horse Winner," in *The Portable D. H. Lawrence,* ed. Diana Trilling (New York: Viking Press, 1946), pp. 148–49.
2. These statistics were taken from the interpretive materials for "One Great Hour of Sharing," a special offering in which the Presbyterian Church (U.S.A.) participates.

Come and See

1. I am grateful to the Rev. David A. Matthew, my friend and colleague in ministry, for suggesting this approach to this passage.

Someone in the Crowd

1. Fred B. Craddock, *Luke* (Louisville, Ky.: Westminster/John Knox Press, 1990), 163.
2. "There's a Spirit in the Air," *The Presbyterian Hymnal* (Louisville, Ky.: Westminster/John Knox Press, 1990), 433.

Bibliography

RESOURCES FOR PREACHING STEWARDSHIP

Ronald J. Allen. "Preaching about Stewardship." In *Preaching In and Out of Season*, ed. Thomas G. Long and Neely Dixon McCarter, 104–17. Louisville, Ky.: Westminster/John Knox Press, 1990.

Kennon L. Callahan. *Effective Church Finances: Fund-Raising and Budgeting for Church Leaders*. New York: HarperCollins, 1992.

———. *Giving and Stewardship in an Effective Church: A Guide for Every Member*. New York: HarperCollins, 1992.

Fred B. Craddock. "Preaching about Giving Thanks." In *Preaching In and Out of Season*, ed. Thomas G. Long and Neely Dixon McCarter, 118–29. Louisville, Ky.: Westminster/John Knox Press, 1990.

Jacques Ellul. *Money and Power*. Downers Grove, Ill.: InterVarsity Press, 1984.

P. C. Enniss. "Preaching Stewardship in an Affluent Congregation." *Journal for Preachers* 18, no. 2 (Lent 1995): 3–8.

Richard J. Foster. *Money, Sex, and Power*. New York: Harper & Row, 1985.

B. A. Gerrish. *Grace and Gratitude: The Eucharistic Theology of John Calvin*. Minneapolis: Fortress Press, 1993.

Justo L. Gonzalez. *Faith and Wealth: A History of Early Christian Ideas on the Origin, Significance, and Use of Money*. New York: Harper & Row, 1990.

Eugene Grimm. *Generous People: How to Encourage Vital Stewardship*. Nashville: Abingdon Press, 1992.

Douglas John Hall. *Christian Mission: The Stewardship of Life in the Kingdom of Death*. New York: Friendship Press, 1985.

———. *The Steward: A Biblical Symbol Come of Age*. New York: Friendship Press, 1982.

Dean Hoge, Charles Zech, Patrick McNamara, and Michael Donahue. *Money Matters: Personal Giving in American Churches*. Louisville, Ky.: Westminster John Knox Press, 1996.

Kevin Jackson, ed. *The Oxford Book of Money*. New York: Oxford University Press, 1995.

Douglas W. Johnson. *The Tithe: Challenge or Legalism?* Nashville: Abingdon Press, 1984.

Patricia Kastner-Wilson. *Preaching Stewardship: An Every-Sunday Theme*. New York: Office of Stewardship, Episcopal Church Center.

John F. Kavanaugh. *Following Christ in a Consumer Society: The Spirituality of Cultural Resistance*. Rev. ed. Maryknoll, N.Y.: Orbis Books, 1991.

Christopher Levan. *The Dancing Steward: Exploring Christian Stewardship Lifestyles*. Toronto: United Church Publishing House, 1993.

W. Robert McClelland. *Worldly Spirituality: Biblical Reflections on Money, Politics, and Sex*. St. Louis, Mo.: CBP Press, 1990.

M. Douglas Meeks. *God the Economist: The Doctrine of God and Political Economy*. Minneapolis: Fortress Press, 1989.

Nordan C. Murphy, ed. *Teaching and Preaching Stewardship: An Anthology*. New York: Friendship Press, 1985.

John Ronsvalle and Sylvia Ronsvalle. *Behind the Stained Glass Windows: Money Dynamics in the Church*. Grand Rapids: Baker Book House, 1996.

Max L. Stackhouse. *Public Theology and Political Economy: Christian Stewardship in Modern Society*. Grand Rapids: Wm. B. Eerdmans Publishing Co., 1987.

W. Taylor Stevenson. *Soul and Money: A Theology of Wealth*. New York: Office of Stewardship, Episcopal Church Center, 1991.

Ronald E. Vallet. *Stepping Stones of the Steward*. Grand Rapids: Wm. B. Eerdmans Publishing Co., 1989.

J. Michael Walker. "Stewardship: From Grace to Gratitude." *Journal for Preachers* 13, no. 1 (Advent 1989): 24–30.

William H. Willimon. "The Effusiveness of Christian Charity." *Theology Today* 49, no. 1 (April 1992): 75–81.

Robert Wuthnow. *God and Mammon in America*. New York: Free Press, 1994.

Robert Wuthnow, Virginia Hodgkinson, et al. *Faith and Philanthropy in America*. San Francisco: Jossey-Bass Publishers, 1990.

SPECIAL ISSUES OF JOURNALS

"Preaching Stewardship." *Journal of Stewardship* 47 (1995).

"Wealth and Poverty in Biblical Perspective." *Interpretation* 41, no. 4 (October 1987).

ORGANIZATIONS

Ecumenical Center for Stewardship Studies
1100 West 42nd Street, Suite 225
Indianapolis, IN   46208-3383
Phone: 317-926-3525
Fax: 317-926-3521

Ministry of Money
2 Professional Drive, Suite 220
Gaithersburg, MD   20879
Phone: 301-670-9606